Practicing Discipleship

Practicing Discipleship

Lived Theologies of Nonviolence in Conversation with the Doctrine of the United Methodist Church

NICOLE L. JOHNSON

PICKWICK *Publications* · Eugene, Oregon

PRACTICING DISCIPLESHIP
Lived Theologies of Nonviolence in Conversation with the Doctrine of the United
Methodist Church

Pickwick Publications
A Division of Wipf and Stock Publishers
199 W. 8th Ave., Suite 3
Eugene, OR 97401

www.wipfandstock.com

ISBN 13: 978-1-60608-009-2

Cataloging-in-Publication data:

Johnson, Nicole L.

　　Practicing discipleship : lived theologies of nonviolence in conversation with the
doctrine of the United Methodist Church / Nicole L. Johnson.

　　　viii + 152 p. ; 23 cm. —Includes bibliographical references.

　　　ISBN 13: 978-1-60608-009-2

　　　1. Peace—Religious aspects—Methodist Church. 2. Methodist Church—
Doctrines. I. Title.

BX8349.P43 J63 2009

Manufactured in the U.S.A.

Contents

Acknowledgments

THIS PROJECT OWES ITS existence to so many people who have, either directly or indirectly, been a part of this work. At Boston University School of Theology, Claire E. Wolfteich and Dale P. Andrews served as first and second readers, respectively, on the dissertation. Their critiques, suggestions, and cheerleading were indispensable in developing and completing this project. Nancy T. Ammerman, Bruce Fraser, John Hart, Zina Jacque, Glen A. Messer, Rodney Petersen, Tom Porter, Bryan P. Stone, and Karen Westerfield Tucker provided insight and encouragement at different stages of this project; in addition, conversations with fellow Th.D. students, particularly Carolynne Brown, Julian Gotobed, and Pat McLeod, offered not only wisdom but also collegiality during the long and lonely months of research and writing. Of course, I would never even have gone on to doctoral studies if it weren't for the virtual *insistence* of my dear friend, mentor, and teacher, John L. McLaughlin, formerly of Wheeling Jesuit University and now of the University of St. Michael's College in Toronto. Most recently, I am indebted to Charlie Collier at Wipf & Stock Publishers for his support of this project.

My sister Julie once used the metaphor of tools in a toolbox to describe the set of skills, gifts, and aptitudes a person receives in her or his life for use in overcoming obstacles and pursuing one's goals. I am blessed with a family (of the immediate, extended, and in-law persuasions) that has provided me with such tools as support, varied and sundry models of faithfulness, a strong work ethic, hilarity and humor, cheerleading, shoulders to cry on, constructive criticism, and unfathomable love throughout my life. One might think that the sheer number and variety of these tools might make for a cumbersome load to lug around from year to year, but in fact these things only make my journey all the lighter and more enjoyable. Words can never express just how grateful I am for my diverse and wonderful family.

Perhaps most of all, this study owes its existence to my husband Glenn, who provided daily doses of laughter (read: sanity), kept up faith in me even when I was drowning in self-doubt, and bore the brunt of my "grumpy days" which occurred regularly with the approach of various deadlines. Glenn has never questioned my academic or career pursuits and has supported me in countless ways. I am so grateful to God for the gift that Glenn is in my life and for this ever-eye-opening journey called "marriage." May the love that we share never cease to surprise and delight.

Finally, without the witness and work of the twelve Methodist individuals who participated in this study, the project simply could not have happened. While I cannot name these twelve friends at this time due to the study's boundaries of confidentiality, what I can reveal is that this dynamic dozen—which includes lay and clergy, male and female, twenty-somethings and long-time AARP members, New Englanders, southerners, and the in-between-ers, and a lovely bouquet of colorful faces—serve a diversity of congregations and communities and are seeking, in their own corners of the world, to make their lives look a little less violent and a little more like Jesus Christ. This book is dedicated to these twelve people. May their witness bring the church to ever-greater faithfulness to God.

1

Introduction

STATEMENT OF THE PROBLEM

IN MARCH 2003, THE United States initiated military action in Iraq. That same month, the United Methodist News Service disseminated an article entitled "Social Principles spell out church's stand on war."[1] Beginning with the observation that "many United Methodists are wondering where their denomination stands on the issue of war," the article admits that although the Social Principles of the United Methodist Church describe war as "incompatible with the teachings of Christ," the denomination "acknowledges that when peaceful alternatives have failed, armed force may be necessary."

Exploration into the United Methodist *Book of Discipline* demonstrates that when it comes to questions about war, peace, and nonviolence, the church is less clear than the title of the News Service article implies and in fact maintains a plurality of views on the topic. Some statements appear within the *Discipline* that seem to posit the United Methodist Church as a pacifist church, while other statements seem to outline a more just war approach. A person attempting to discern how she should respond to the moral dilemma of war and violence would find conflicting teachings, depending on the part of the doctrine to which she looked.

While parts of the *Discipline* do seem to promote nonviolence, relative to statements that more clearly espouse just war teachings, nonviolence is certainly a minority view.[2] In addition, there can be little argument

1. United Methodist News Service, "Social Principles spell out church's stand on war," March 20, 2003, http://dev.umns.umc.org/03/mar/160.htm.

2. In his study of 491 United Methodist conscientious objectors during the Vietnam War, S. Ronald Parks argues that "Support for the pacifist minority has been expressed in the official pronouncements of the church but seldom promoted by the programmatic

that a vast majority of Methodists in the United States would not identify themselves as pacifist or nonviolent.[3] Despite this fact and despite the general lack of clarity within United Methodist doctrine around issues of war and peace, some United Methodist persons take a particular stand on the moral issue of war by developing and sustaining a commitment to nonviolence that they understand as central to Christian faith.

How and why do some United Methodists come to this commitment in a denomination that doctrinally and practically is not considered to be a pacifist church? For those who see nonviolence as central to Christian faith, what are the theological beliefs and practices that underwrite that commitment, and how might this minority voice shape one's thinking about United Methodist doctrine and teachings about war and non-violence? In an effort to draw out this minority voice within the United Methodist Church, and in the hope of contributing to current conversations about war and nonviolence in the denomination and beyond it, this study seeks to answer the following questions: *What is the lived theology of United Methodist Christians who are committed to nonviolence, and what sustains that commitment? How might a lived theology of nonviolence speak to a denomination that maintains a plurality of teachings within its doctrinal tradition?*

SIGNIFICANCE OF THE STUDY

How one should interpret doctrinal plurality on a given moral issue—in this case, the issue of war and violence—is a significant question for this study. On one hand, such plurality may yield confusion and incoherence within the denomination. That confusion exists in the church on this is-

---

agencies of the denomination." As he also notes in the study: "The legacy of the CO [conscientious objector] in United Methodism has been a story of dissenters adopting a position that the majority of Methodists have valued but not supported. Traditionally the United Methodist Church has espoused a just-war ethic. That stance has let it support the government's war efforts while maintaining that war itself is an affront to both God and humanity. Therefore the United Methodist CO has had to stand not only against the call for combatant service but also against the church's endorsement of each military campaign." Parks, "Free (but Not Helped) to Be Pacifist."

3. The Council of Bishops itself states that "The courage and endurance of the pacifist tradition have not prevented most Christians and virtually all governments from appealing to nonpacifist principles in support of military establishments and the resort to war. For many Christians the principle that matters most has been obedience to whatever their government demands." United Methodist Council of Bishops, *In Defense of Creation*, 32.

sue is evident in the diversity of views contained in United Methodist News articles distributed prior to the start of the war in Iraq.[4] On the other hand, such pluralism may be appropriate to Methodism, which is in part characterized by a sense of inclusion and openness to the leading of the Spirit within a diverse community of faith. As the *Book of Discipline* states, Methodists live and worship together "in a covenant of grace"[5] wherein "Devising formal definitions of doctrine has been less pressing … than summoning people to faith and nurturing them in the knowledge and love of God."[6] However, after pointing to the long legacy of Methodist social concern and to "the connection between doctrine and ethics," the *Discipline* also confirms that conflicting teachings on ethical issues are problematic because "a church lacking the courage to act decisively on personal and social issues loses its claim to moral authority."[7]

In seeking to answer the central research question regarding the lived theology of nonviolence and how that commitment is sustained, it is critical to understand what accounts for the beliefs and practices of contemporary United Methodists around questions of war and nonviolence. This project attends to one part of this issue by exploring the lived theology of those United Methodists who have arrived at a commitment to nonviolence. This particular approach to thinking about nonviolence in the United Methodist Church will build upon but move beyond the work of theologians who want to call the church to a pacifist stance based primarily on the pacifist-oriented statements in United Methodist doctrine. While an effort to highlight these doctrinal statements is an important contribution to the conversation, existing scholarship has yet to explore the lived theology of those who strive to sustain a commitment to nonviolence in the United Methodist Church. By highlighting the voices of contemporary United Methodist Christians who make an explicit and

4. The confusion is evident in the titles of the articles, all of which are found on the website of the United Methodist News Service, http://umns.umc.org: "Pastor, friend of Bush's, supports president on Iraq," November 4, 2002; "Commentary: Methodists are called to witness for peace," by C. Dale White, December 19, 2002; "Bishops' president urges Bush to use restraint with Iraq," February 6, 2003; "Commentary: War now would not be justifiable" by Joseph Allen, 20 February 2003; "Commentary: For Christians, every war is a civil war" by Peter Storey, February 20, 2003; "Commentary: Just cause exists for action against Iraq" by Donald Sensing, February 20, 2003.

5. *Book of Discipline* (2004), 41.

6. Ibid., 50.

7. Ibid., 49.

intentional commitment to nonviolence, this study contributes to wider conversations in the church as it grapples with issues of war and nonviolence. This grappling has been noted above and is further demonstrated by the changes since 1972 to the United Methodist Social Principles which address war, military service, and pacifism. As textual analysis will show, continual changes to the statements on "Military Service" and "War and Peace" suggest that the problem of how the church should respond to questions of war and peace is far from settled. It is hoped that the lives and work of those who are both United Methodist and committed to nonviolence would provide wisdom which might speak to the denomination as it seeks to be faithful to its calling as a church which follows Christ.

This project's emphasis on lived theology points to the interrelatedness of belief and practice in the lives of those who maintain a commitment to nonviolence. The project explores the theological *sources* and *beliefs* that undergird such a commitment. Upon what, if any, authoritative Christian sources (such as Scripture, theology, church history, and historical theology)[8] does the nonviolent community rely? What other theories and ideas do people view as foundational to their commitments to nonviolence? At the same time, the project explores the specific *practices* of nonviolence within the particularities of the lives of contemporary United Methodist Christians. What are the practices in which those who understand themselves to be nonviolent engage? How do Christians who hold to an ethic of nonviolence define and understand those practices? What are the practices that sustain the practitioner in his or her efforts? And how do beliefs and practices of nonviolence come together to shape the nonviolent commitment and way of life? As Craig Dykstra has argued, it is in the engagement of practices that we are moved to greater commitment: "People come to faith and grow in the life of faith in the context of these practices as they themselves, participating in them actively, actually do what these practices involve."[9]

---

8. Browning, "Toward a Fundamental and Strategic Practical Theology," 304. Elsewhere Browning expands on these "classic sources that have shaped our present practices. The classic sources are generally religio-cultural texts and monuments. For Christians these texts and monuments are the Scriptures, the Hebrew and Greek sources that have informed them, and the major texts and monuments that have shaped the Christian tradition down through the ages." Browning, *Fundamental Practical Theology*, 39.

9. Dykstra, *Growing in the Life of Faith*, 44.

The project also looks closely at the relationship between doctrinal teachings and the beliefs and practices of those who do not exactly agree with those teachings. How people name and negotiate their disagreements with integrity while remaining very active in and connected to the United Methodist Church is a particularly important aspect of the study. How do those in the minority on a given issue—in this case, those who commit to a nonviolent ethic—find support in the church and even grow in their commitments despite the fact that those commitments are not part of the mainstream thinking, doctrinally or practically, of the church?

Finally, this study has strong potential to offer to the church creative suggestions for how it might be more faithful to its nature and mission as a body that follows the "Prince of Peace." Is the lived theology of nonviolence, as it is understood and practiced by nonviolent United Methodists, convincing and persuasive to other United Methodists as a valid and viable moral option for a Christian person to choose? If so, how might that lived theology of nonviolence challenge a denomination that seems uncertain in its teaching around war, violence, and nonviolence? It is assumed in this study that there is something to be learned on the part of the larger denomination from those who maintain a commitment to Christian nonviolence. The author hopes that in giving a hearing to those for whom nonviolence is a key expression of Christian faith, the United Methodist Church would gain insight into how the church might respond most faithfully to the pressing moral issues of war and violence.

INTENDED AUDIENCE

Three different audiences exist for this study: the academy, the United Methodist Church, and the wider Christian church. The project contributes to the field of Practical Theology by posing a method of theological research and reflection that takes very seriously the beliefs and practices of people who are attempting to live out their understandings of Christian faith in concrete and meaningful ways. In so doing, the project proposes that attention to what "real people" actually think and do has the potential to revitalize the church and provide much-needed direction for ecclesial life, especially as this life is expressed in the church's doctrine, ethics, and efforts toward faith-formation of its members. The method of practical-theological reflection utilized in this study does not *necessarily* give primacy to the lived theology over and against the doctrinal tradition, but draws both into a constructive dialogue in pursuit of what it might mean for the church to practice and exhibit a greater faithfulness.

By taking this lived-theology approach, the project contributes to current academic research trends in lived theology and its related variations such as lived religion, everyday theologies, and lay theology.[10] In doing so, the project raises fundamental questions about how theological reflection is carried out by challenging the assumption that one can know what a person believes based solely on his or her church's doctrine and teachings. Members of churches do not always adopt the teachings of their traditions as absolute truth; rather, they reason theologically based on their own interpretations of authoritative theological sources and also on their own experience and reason. A lived theology approach recognizes the wisdom and value to be discovered within the lives of everyday Christian people.

Also with regard to the field of Practical Theology, the study models one way of navigating the relationship between social science research methods—namely, a phenomenologically-oriented qualitative methodology—and practical-theological discovery; in this case, the study positions social science research methods *in service to* the larger practical-theological (and Christian) enterprise, viewing such methods as important tools particularly for the purpose of elucidating and describing the views of nonviolent United Methodist Christians. As Swinton and Mowat argue, "Practical Theology is *theological* reflection" and therefore "theology is (or at least should be) the primary source of knowledge which guides and provides the hermeneutical framework within which Practical Theology carries out its task."[11] While this position does not preclude the importance of "critical reflection and challenge" to theology, it assumes that "While there remains much scope for critical dialogue and mutual reflection, the conversation is always inherently asymmetrical with theology having necessary logical priority."[12] Given the researcher's understanding of the

---

10. Evidence of increased interest in lived theology and its related variations abounds. See, for example, the following recent studies: Hall, *Lived Religion in America: Toward a History of Practice*; Moon, *God, Sex, and Politics: Homosexuality and Everyday Theologies*; Ammerman, *Everyday Religion: Observing Modern Religious Lives*; and Vanhoozer, Anderson, and Sleasman, *Everyday Theology: How to Read Cultural Texts and Interpret Trends*. See also the website for "The Project on Lived Theology" at the University of Virginia: http://www.livedtheology.org/.

11. Swinton and Mowat, *Practical Theology and Qualitative Research*, 7.

12. Ibid., 88.

task of Practical Theology "to 'remind' the Church of the subtle ways in which it differs from the world and to ensure that its practices remain faithful to the script of the gospel,"[13] for the purposes and direction of the current study, at least, the researcher agrees with Swinton and Mowat that "Practical Theology can utilize qualitative research methods to aid in this process of ensuring that Christian practice is in correspondence to the event of God's self-communication."[14]

The second audience is the United Methodist Church and the different levels that constitute it. At the denominational level, the General Board of Church and Society is charged with the responsibility to "seek the implementation of the Social Principles" and to "conduct a program of research, education, and action on the wide range of issues that confront the Church."[15] The General Board of Discipleship works to "provide resources that support growth in Christian discipleship."[16] This study seeks an audience with both of these General Boards so as to contribute to denominational conversations about faithfulness to God in questions of war and peace.

The project also seeks an audience with the wider United Methodist Church as it deals with issues related to doctrinal pluralism. In wrestling with the potential benefits and negative ramifications of such pluralism, the study challenges the denomination to consider its doctrine more carefully and to continue to struggle with its role in and meaning for the church.

Local congregations might wish to use the study in discussions about how to respond to critical issues of war and violence. Assuming that many United Methodists would be rather surprised to learn what the *Book of Discipline* actually says, the study would at least provide a better knowledge of their doctrinal statements and might serve as a point of departure for discussions about church teachings and witness. It is hoped too that individuals would be moved to think through their own views and commitments, and that they would be challenged by the nonviolent witness of fellow United Methodist believers who are seeking to live out their faith convictions in concrete ways.

---

13. Ibid., 9.
14. Ibid., 90–91.
15. *Book of Discipline* (2004), 512–13.
16. Ibid., 516.

Finally, the author of this study hopes that non-Methodist ecclesial bodies would find value in the project as well. Obviously ecclesial bodies differ from one another in terms of ecclesial polity, authority, and organization and would need to adjust the study to fit those parameters appropriately. However, questions of war and peace are critical moral issues, and the witness of the churches in confronting societal evils seems a particularly important challenge given the current political climate both at home and abroad. This study's author suspects that within other major ecclesial bodies in the United States, there exist pockets of nonviolent members whose theological beliefs and practices may have something very important to communicate to their respective ecclesial traditions. Similar studies of other churches' doctrinal statements and the lifting up of nonviolence as a viable and valid Christian response within those churches would be a welcome extension of this project's research.

DEFINITIONS

Located within the central research questions identified above are a few key terms that require definition: *nonviolence, lived theology,* and *practice.*

"Nonviolence" is defined in relationship to the associated term "pacifism." While the two are often used inter-changeably, the researcher understands the latter more specifically as a political term that refers to a consistent refusal to participate in war and other forms of government-sanctioned violence. The former refers more broadly to a way of life that eschews violence in all its forms and that would thus normally assume pacifism as a response to the particular issue of participating in war. Neither term is intended to suggest a passive-ness in the face of violent struggle or conflict; in fact, what is assumed in both definitions is a strong commitment to active social concern and engagement in and with the world. In addition, the researcher differentiates from *radical* nonviolence, which would not permit the use of violence even in defense of self or of an innocent. While such a radical commitment is not ruled out in selecting participants for the qualitative aspect of the study, it is not a requirement of participation.

"Lived theology" is understood as the cumulative theological practices, values, ideals, and principles which constitute and sustain the faith commitments of an individual or community. More specifically, a lived theology of nonviolence would include the practices and principles that constitute and sustain the commitments to Christian nonviolence in the life of an individual or community. In order to understand such lived theology, reflection must occur that makes explicit those practices and principles that are constitutive of that theology.

For the purpose of defining "practice," works by Craig Dykstra and Dorothy C. Bass are particularly insightful. Drawing on the work of Alasdair MacIntyre, Dykstra asserts that

> practices are those cooperative human activities through which we, as individuals and as communities, grow and develop in moral character and substance. They have built up over time and, through experience and testing, have developed patterns of reciprocal expectations among participants. They are ways of doing things together in which and through which human life is given direction, meaning, and significance, and through which our very capacities to do good things well are increased.[17]

Similarly, Dorothy Bass defines practices as "patterns of cooperative human activity in and through which life together takes shape over time in response to and in the light of God as known in Jesus Christ."[18] In sum, "practice" can be defined as any activity performed by an individual or community that is repetitive over time, intentional, and constitutive of a particular way of life—in the case of this project, the nonviolent way of life.

LIMITATIONS

In order to limit the scope and size of this project, it has been confined to a particular denomination in a particular country: the United Methodist Church in the United States. It is hoped, however, that this project might serve as an invitation or a point of departure for other church bodies that are wrestling with how to address questions of war, peace, and nonviolence in the contemporary world. The realities of war and violence pose urgent questions for all Christian churches today, and, as expressed above, replications of this study by other denominations and groups are encouraged by the researcher.

The extent to which textual analysis will be conducted has been limited in order to keep the study focused and manageable. This study

17. Dykstra, *Growing in the Life of Faith*, 69–70.
18. Volf and Bass, *Practicing Theology*, 3.

is not meant to provide an exhaustive analysis of textual changes nor of the development of church teachings throughout Methodist history. Textual analysis will cover United Methodist teachings since its inception in 1968 and will include an analysis of Article XVI of the Evangelical United Brethren Church's Confession of Faith. The project also does not look at other sources of United Methodist teaching and guidance, such as the Council of Bishops or church hymnody. While both are important and contribute to the peace movement within the United Methodist Church, these sources do not carry the level of authority that the *Book of Discipline*, as the "law" of the church, holds.

Other limitations involve the very nature of qualitative interviewing, which depends on the self-reporting, memory, and interpretation of the interviewee-participant. In addition, interview data can be distorted by the interviewer's biases, presuppositions, and anxiety or other emotions.[19] Patton suggests, however, that this kind of qualitative data can provide "in-depth responses about people's experiences, perceptions, opinions, feelings, and knowledge."[20] Such in-depth responses provide insight into the lived theology of United Methodist Christians who are committed to nonviolence.

A potential limitation of the qualitative process used in this particular project involves the use of "snowball" or "chain" sampling which, instead of providing a random sample, identifies potential interviewees by asking people for names of others who might be good sources for this study.[21] Such sampling depends on the knowledge and relationships of "well-situated"[22] people in a particular area of inquiry. However, this allows the researcher to identify potential interviewees who fit within a certain frame of reference (in this case, United Methodist Christians with a commitment to nonviolence). It is a type of purposeful sampling that provides "information-rich cases—cases from which one can learn a great deal about matters of importance and therefore worthy of in-depth study."[23]

---

19. Patton, *Qualitative Research and Evaluation Methods*, 306.

20. Ibid., 4.

21. Ibid., 243.

22. Ibid., 237.

23. Ibid., 242.

Another potential limitation of the qualitative process is located in the sample size. In order to complete the project in a reasonable amount of time, the sample consists of twelve in-depth interviews. Because the qualitative aspect of the study is intended to generate some initial dialogue between the lived theology of practitioners of nonviolence and United Methodist teachings about war and peace, interviews with twelve information-rich cases provide sufficient data for beginning to think about the questions raised in this study.

Finally, the study does not address multiple forms of violence such as domestic violence, gang violence, or police force and other various types of government-sanctioned violence. Both the analysis of United Methodist statements and the questions asked during the qualitative interviews are limited to those statements and questions that are concerned with war as a specific form of violence. This parameter provides focus and manageability in the study.

LOCATION OF THE RESEARCHER

Currently, the researcher would not self-identify as a resolutely non-violent United Methodist Christian. At the same time, the researcher recognizes within herself a profound respect for past and present practitioners of nonviolence and a strong attraction to the nonviolent witness—and also wonders what kind of faith and discipleship is required to sustain that commitment in a world that overwhelmingly seems to view nonviolence as weak and irresponsible. This study arises out of an honest and inquisitive desire to explore the commitment to nonviolence through the lives of those who live it, to examine it as a viable and valid moral option, and to consider its place in the life and witness of the United Methodist Church.

2

Research Methodology

OVERVIEW

IN ORDER TO ADDRESS the central research questions named in the Introduction, this project aims to draw out the lived theology of nonviolence in the United Methodist Church and to bring it into dialogue with the doctrinal teachings on war, peace, and nonviolence. To this end, the study moves through four main stages. The first stage is a review of relevant literature which frames the specific research questions and guides the project's interpretations, discoveries, and conclusions (chapter 3). The second stage consists of an analysis of selected statements on war, peace, and nonviolence contained within the *Book of Disciple of the United Methodist Church* and the *Book of Resolutions of the United Methodist Church* (chapter 4). Third, the project moves to qualitative analysis of in-depth interviews with United Methodist Christians who are committed to nonviolence (chapter 5). Finally, the doctrinal teachings and the lived theology are brought into a dialogue in which the lived theology of nonviolence is given the opportunity to challenge the doctrine (and thereby the wider United Methodist Church) by encouraging it, in line with a primary goal of practical-theological reflection,[1] to wrestle with what it means to be a more faithful church (chapter 6).

LITERATURE REVIEW

The review of relevant literature in chapter 3 provides important foundations for the overall study. First, the review helps to locate the project within a wider ethical framework by juxtaposing nonviolence with what

1. Swinton and Mowat, *Practical Theology and Qualitative Research*, 7; Cobb and Hough, *Christian Identity and Theological Education*, 18, 126.

is generally thought to be its alternative, the just war tradition. Second, the review notes the range of existing theologies of nonviolence and gives evidence of the prevailing mode of reflection on nonviolence, which moves from theology to prescription without any reference to how nonviolence is perceived and practiced by real people. Third, the review highlights scholarship on "lived" theology and religion in order to guide the project's intention to move beyond a more applied model of theological reflection. Finally, the review explores scholarship that introduces the topic of doctrinal pluralism and consistency, which is addressed more explicitly in later chapters. Taken together, the scholarship reviewed in chapter 3 situates the project within a wider body of knowledge, provides shape and direction for the project, and prepares the way for deeper theological reflection later in the book. Much of the literature will be revisited in the following chapters.

TEXTUAL METHODOLOGY

Guiding the life and work of the contemporary United Methodist Church are two written sources of doctrine and teaching: the *Book of Discipline of the United Methodist Church* and the *Book of Resolutions of the United Methodist Church*. The *Discipline* is divided into five major sections: the Constitution; the Doctrinal Standards and General Rules; a statement on the "Ministry of All Christians"; the Social Principles; and a lengthy section on the "Organization and Administration" of the church. While the *Discipline* is described as the "book of law" of the United Methodist Church, it is not considered to be "sacrosanct or infallible." The *Discipline* "is the most current statement of how United Methodists agree to live their lives together. It reflects our understanding of the Church and of what is expected of its laity and clergy as they seek to be effective witnesses in the world as a part of the whole body of Christ." The General Conference, which meets every four years, "amends, perfects, clarifies, and adds its own contribution to the *Discipline*."[2]

The General Conference alone reserves the right to speak for the church.[3] Included in the permanent record of each General Conference is the *Book of Resolutions*, which contains "all valid resolutions of the

---

2. *Book of Discipline* (2004), v. Also Waltz, *Dictionary for United Methodists*, 81–82.
3. Ibid., 317.

General Conference."[4] These resolutions "state the policy of The United Methodist Church on many current social issues and concerns."[5] They are understood as the "official policy statements for guiding all the work and ministry of The United Methodist Church on approximately 200 subjects."[6] They are also understood as "educational resources" around pertinent issues, "guides and models" that help people live more faithfully, and "resource materials."[7] In the words of one source, the resolutions are "considered to represent the position of The United Methodist Church. The text of any resolution is considered the official position of the denomination on that subject."[8]

Scott Jones provides helpful insight into how the different aspects of United Methodist doctrine should be understood authoritatively. Jones divides United Methodist doctrine into three levels. The first and highest level of authority includes "constitutional standards," which consist of the Constitution, the Articles of Religion, the Confession of Faith, the General Rules, and John Wesley's *Sermons* and *Explanatory Notes on the New Testament*. The second level includes the "nonconstitutional sections" of the *Discipline* (which includes the Social Principles) and the *Book of Resolutions*. The third level includes the *United Methodist Hymnal* and the *United Methodist Book of Worship*.[9]

In the textual analysis to be pursued in the following chapter, I will be dealing, then, with parts of United Methodist doctrine that fall into the first and second levels of authority. Article XVI of the Evangelical United Brethren Confession of Faith is part of the first level of authority; it will be treated in the analysis precisely because it has been claimed as a key source for those theologians who claim the United Methodist Church as constitutionally pacifist. At the second level of authority, the analysis will deal with statements from the Social Principles that attempt to spell out most explicitly the church's position on war and nonviolence: "War and Peace" and "Military Service." The analysis will trace the changes to these principles by General Conference since the inception of the United Methodist

---

4. Ibid., 318.

5. *Book of Resolutions of the United Methodist Church* (2004), 5.

6. Ibid., 23.

7. Ibid., 23.

8. Waltz, *Dictionary for United Methodists*, 161.

9. Jones, *United Methodist Doctrine*, 47.

Church in 1968. Finally, as "amplifications" of the Social Principles[10] and as representative of the ongoing conversation of the church on contemporary moral concerns, selected resolutions[11] that deal with war and peace will be included in the textual analysis. Again, additions, deletions, and significant changes since 1968 will be noted. With regard to the two Social Principles statements and the selected resolutions to be considered, some context, where available, will be provided with reference to the General Conference Journals that correspond to particular changes.

In the textual analysis, United Methodist doctrine will be plumbed for statements, documents, and resolutions that address war, peace, and nonviolence. The intention is to understand what, exactly, the United Methodist denomination says and teaches about these issues. The claim at this juncture is that such an investigation will yield a multiplicity of views, raising questions about what such multiplicity means in a denomination. At best, doctrinal plurality on a particular issue may be indicative of an "open" church that welcomes all views into the fray as it wrestles with difficult questions; at worst, it is a sign of doctrinal uncertainty which may lead to confusion within the United Methodist Church around tremendously important moral issues. In order to struggle with this question, the project turns to a qualitatively-based inquiry of those representing the minority voice on the issue of war and violence: namely, those individuals who have committed to a nonviolent ethic and lifestyle.

QUALITATIVE METHODOLOGY

Phenomenological Orientation

This study seeks an understanding of the lived theologies and expressions of nonviolence on the part of those who hold that commitment as central to Christian faith. Stated another way, the research focuses on the commitment to nonviolence as a particular phenomenon for study; therefore the qualitative methods utilized for the project are phenomenological in orientation. Phenomenology asks, "What is the meaning, structure, and essence of the lived experience of this phenomenon for this group

10. *Book of Resolutions* (1968), 5.

11. To study comprehensively and exhaustively the changes to the *Book of Resolutions* since 1968—even with regard to this one topic—would constitute its own dissertation. A selected sampling of more significant changes to the *Resolutions* will suffice to support the point.

of people?"[12] Seeking to understand this "lived experience" allows the researcher to understand the lived theology of an individual who identifies as a practitioner of Christian nonviolence.

In a phenomenological study, in-depth interviews usually serve as the primary source of information. Such interviews allow the researcher to understand the lived experience of the phenomenon by listening carefully to the insights, stories, and views of people who have experienced the phenomenon.[13] In this study, data for arriving at an understanding of what comprises the lived theology of nonviolence among United Methodists derive from interviews with individuals who self-identify as having a commitment to nonviolence. Questions that seek to answer what insights, experiences, and normative sources are used in constructing and maintaining that commitment yield data that allow the researcher to see the "meaning, structure, and essence" of the lived theology of nonviolence within the lives of United Methodist Christians.

Data Collection

Participant Selection

SELECTION CRITERIA. The criteria for participant involvement in the study were fairly straightforward. First, participants had to self-identify as "nonviolent"[14] and had to be identifiable by others as such. Second, in order to include the perspectives of those whose identity is shaped by United Methodism, only those individuals who had been a member of the church for at least ten years were selected.[15] Finally, a very intentional

---

12. Patton, *Qualitative Research and Evaluation Methods*, 104.

13. Ibid., 106; Creswell, *Qualitative Inquiry and Research Design*, 54.

14. The researcher resisted defining for potential interviewees what she meant by "nonviolence" because how United Methodist Christians understand and define their own commitments is a key aspect of the qualitative interviews. In addition, the criteria for what might constitute a "commitment" to nonviolence were intentionally left undefined because such a commitment can be demonstrated in many ways, including paid and volunteer work, activities and associations, and lifestyle.

15. This criterion was modified slightly in two of the twelve cases. In one case, the participant's relative youth meant that while he had been closely involved in the United Methodist Church for ten years, he had been a member only for six. In the second case, the participant was a Methodist from South America who had been in the United States for only five years. However in those five years, her clergy status and her leadership at both the denominational and local levels had connected her in significant ways to the United Methodist Church in the United States, giving her the time and experience needed to be able to reflect thoughtfully and critically on the church.

effort was made to diversify in terms of gender, age, race, lay or clergy status, geographical location, and organizational affiliation, if any.

SELECTION PROCESS. Participants were located through a process of chain or "snowball" sampling, which allows the researcher to locate "information-rich" subjects by first asking "well-situated people"[16] (also known as "key informants") for names of individuals who might fit the specified criteria for participation. In April 2006, the selection process began with phone calls to key informants already known to the researcher; these individuals were asked for the names of three to five people who might fit the selection criteria and who might be interested in participating in the study. These first key informants included United Methodist bishops, clergy, and laypersons known for their work in peace-making, social justice, and social concerns. By phone and/or email, the researcher contacted each potential interviewee, described the project, explained the criteria for participation, and invited the individual to participate in the study.

Next, directors of United Methodist-related organizations were contacted by phone or email. With the permission of one organization's director, an informational email was distributed to all area coordinators with an invitation to participate in the project, provided the criteria were a match for that individual. The director of another organization provided the names and contact information of five potential interviewees. Again, these suggested individuals were contacted through follow-up phone calls and emails.

Once a potential participant agreed to an interview, a copy of the Informed Consent Form (Appendix A) was sent to the individual for his or her perusal and prior to final confirmation. If the individual agreed fully to the stipulations of the interview, which included audio-recording, a final confirmation was made by phone or email and a day, time, and place was designated for the interview. The process of contacting individuals continued until a list of twelve[17] participants was finally completed.[18]

16. Patton, *Qualitative Research and Evaluation Methods*, 237.

17. In the initial project proposal, the researcher committed to ten interviews; two extra interviews were added during the participant selection process for a total of twelve interviews.

18. In designing this project, the researcher was certain that the process of finding and selecting interviewees would be one of the easier parts of the dissertation. It would be a serious understatement to say that she was surprised by how time-consuming and frustrating this process really was.

A table of participants, noted by demographic data, is noted below in Table 1.

Table 1: Demographic Summary of Study Participants

GENDER		AGE		RACE		CLERGY/LAY	
Female	6	20–39	4	Black	3	Lay	3
Male	6	40–59	4	Latino/a	2	Clergy (pastor)	6
		60–79	4	White	7	Clergy (non-pastor)	3

Interview Process

All twelve interviews took place between August 6 and September 19 of 2006 and were conducted in-person at the convenience of the interviewee. The interviews lasted from 70 to 90 minutes and were conducted in various locations, including the participant's home, office, or church.

At the start of the interview, participants were asked to re-read and sign an official copy of the Informed Consent Form. Next, participants were asked to complete an Interview Aid (Appendix B) which had a twofold purpose. The top portion asked for demographic information, which is used to identify participants while protecting confidentiality in later chapters. The lower portion listed four very general questions to aid in preparation for the interview; participants were given a maximum of ten minutes to reflect on their commitments to nonviolence including basic definitions, theological foundations, practices, and reflections about United Methodist teachings on war and nonviolence. For those who arrived at the interview following a class, a business meeting, or in one case, a two-week vacation, the Interview Aid served as a centering tool; for others whose work or associations in nonviolence require reflection on an almost constant basis, it was less helpful. Completion of the demographic information was required but completion of the reflection questions was optional as needed.

The actual interview was conducted using a previously prepared Interview Grid (Appendix C) which listed topics and related questions to be addressed with each participant; however, the researcher took care to keep the interview conversational and to allow space for follow-up questions to key insights arising from participants' reflections. Topics focused on the participant's definition and understanding of nonviolence, what theological ideas and values undergird the commitment to nonviolence, how that commitment is practiced in life and work, and how that commitment is sustained within a denomination that does not espouse nonviolence as a normative requirement for membership in the United Methodist Church nor necessary to Christian faith and discipleship.

Management of Data

TRANSCRIPTION AND CORRECTION. All interviews were audio-recorded and transcribed verbatim by a professional transcription company. Each interview was then corrected for errors by the researcher by listening carefully to the interview tape while reading the transcript. This careful listening also provided for the development of additional codes and themes, which were logged in a research memo for convenient retrieval at different phases of data analysis and interpretation.

CONFIDENTIALITY AND STORAGE. All tape recordings were kept in the researcher's home office in a locked box. Informed Consent forms, Interview Aids with demographic information, and Interview Grids with the researcher's interview notes were organized by interview in a binder and kept in a private file cabinet.

Data Analysis

Use of Qualitative Software

Transcripts of the twelve interviews were imported into NVivo 7, a qualitative research software program developed by QSR International which helps the researcher to code, categorize, analyze, and interpret large amounts of qualitative data. While qualitative software can *facilitate* this process, the researcher "must still decide what things go together to form a pattern, what constitutes a theme, what to name it, and what meanings to extract from case studies. The human being, not the software, must decide how to frame a case study, how much and what to include, and how to tell the story."[19]

---

19. Patton, *Qualitative Research and Evaluation Methods*, 442.

Inductive Analysis

The researcher's decisions about what to include and how to organize and understand the data were made through "inductive analysis." The analytical process outlined in the next section describes the steps included in this kind of analysis, which "involves *discovering* patterns, themes, and categories in one's data."[20] To aid in this discovery, phenomenological analysis requires the researcher to spend as much time "living with the data" as can be reasonably spent.[21] This time of immersion in the data allows the data to speak to the researcher and creates the space for new questions, insights, and understanding to develop.

Coding and Categorizing

Prior to and in preparation for actual coding, a list of initial codes, or basic units of description or meaning, was developed. These included codes driven by interview questions, or "pre-codes,"[22] potential codes that were identified during the interviews themselves, and codes identified during the process of listening to and correcting transcripts.

As part of the first stage of analysis, each interview was analyzed systematically. Sections of data, which ranged from a brief phrase to multiple paragraphs, were copied and filed under the appropriate codes within the NVivo 7 software program. As new codes were discovered, they were added to the code list and relevant sections of data were filed accordingly. This process continued until all relevant sections of data from each interview had been assigned a unit of meaning.

At the second stage of analysis, individual codes were grouped into logical categories, called "tree codes." The original research questions were constantly referred to as the basis for the creation of categories; in other words, as groupings become apparent, they were held against the research questions to ensure that the questions were being answered. Outlying codes and categories were noted as such but were retained for the purpose of analysis and reflection at later stages.

20. Ibid., 453.

21. Ibid., 486–87.

22. Many of these question-driven pre-codes actually followed a category-codes-categories analysis. For example, large sections of data were filed under the much larger category of "Practices" and were later parsed into multiple codes listing discreet practices. These discreet practices were then re-grouped into multiple recognizable sub-categories.

Finally, multiple categories were organized into larger groupings for the purpose of attempting to answer the questions posed by the research project. As the point of departure for constructing answers to the central questions, the questions were parsed into more discreet questions; the corresponding categories that would provide answers were matched with the appropriate questions.

Throughout this process, the author kept a set of memos comprising a research journal. As insights, possible connections between data codes and groupings, and critical questions arose, they were recorded in memos for retrieval at further stages of analysis and reflection.

Explication

In the last phase of phenomenological analysis, a researcher brings the findings from the data together in a "creative and meaningful way. *Creative synthesis* is the bringing together of the pieces that have emerged into a total experience, showing patterns and relationships. This phase points the way for new perspectives and meanings, a new vision of the experience. The fundamental richness of the experience and the experiencing participants is captured and communicated in a personal and creative way."[23] The "creative synthesis" of this study's qualitative research is the subject of chapter 5.

PRACTICAL-THEOLOGICAL DIALOGUE

In *Christian Identity and Theological Education*, John Cobb and Joseph Hough suggest that a primary goal of Practical Theology is the continual clarification of what it means to have a distinctly Christian identity as followers of Christ and as participants in the Christian story.[24] To this end, Practical Theology seeks the continual reflection upon and reassessment of the church's use of time, energy, and other resources, which is to be judged according to its identity as the community which tells, re-tells, and remembers the Christian story. Continual reflection on the problem of war and violence and ongoing discernment about how the church should respond to this problem in a way that exhibits faithfulness to the Christian story are critical to recovering and discovering a distinctly Christian faith and identity.

23. Patton, *Qualitative Research and Evaluation Methods*, 487.
24. Cobb and Hough, *Christian Identity and Theological Education*, 18, 126.

In *Foundations for a Practical Theology of Ministry*, James Poling and Donald Miller helpfully suggest "that there are several valid ways of perceiving the discipline of practical theology to which we can each turn as we face different problems in a variety of contexts."[25] These different approaches to practical-theological reflection are not "mutually exclusive and competitive with one another," and which methods we use and foci we emphasize "will simply depend on our goals, context, and resources."[26] This particular project aims to discover what theological insights and practical transformations might occur through theological reflection upon and dialogue between the doctrine and teachings of the United Methodist Church and the lived theology of United Methodists who are committed to nonviolence. Based on this aim, and because the project is one that seeks to challenge the church to wrestle with greater faithfulness to Christ in terms of its response to issues of war and violence, this project adopts a practical-theological framework that is confessional, meaning that it is focused on "interpretation and reinterpretation of the Christian story and tradition and treats this story as normative for today"[27] and is "centered in the practice of a concrete community of Christian faith in mission."[28] While the project does not wish to rule out necessarily the ramifications or the vision for nonviolent practice and witness in the wider society, for the sake of limitation it does hold the church as the primary focus of practical-theological reflection.

The study takes a "lived theology" approach in order to complement the applied model which dominates so much scholarship on Christian nonviolence. To be sure, this approach does not imply that practices of nonviolence are given absolute primacy over theology; in fact, as will be seen in chapter 5 and drawn out in chapter 6, a strong and biblically-based Christocentrism is at the heart of the lived theology of nonviolence. The approach undertaken in this study differs from a strictly applied model in its concern with how real people define, practice, and theologically ground their commitments to nonviolence, particularly in a denomination which does not view that commitment as a requirement of Christian faith or church membership.

---

25. Poling and Miller, *Foundations for a Practical Theology of Ministry*, 30.

26. Ibid., 35.

27. Ibid., 51.

28. Ibid., 57.

In order to answer the central research questions, the project draws into practical-theological dialogue the two main bodies of information: the textual analysis of United Methodist doctrinal statements on war and nonviolence and the lived theology of nonviolence as it emerges from in-depth interviews with twelve nonviolent United Methodists. First, the primary theological groundings of each conversation partner are questioned and briefly assessed. The objective is to disclose the theological crux or center of each position and then to weigh that grounding against the meaning of "discipleship," particularly as it is defined by United Methodist doctrine itself. Next, findings from the qualitative analysis in chapter 5 are brought into dialogue with the doctrinal teachings on war and violence in order to discover some of the specific challenges and insights the lived theology might present to the United Methodist Church and its doctrine. Specific attention will then be given to the question of whether doctrinal pluralism within the United Methodist Church is a source of confusion, and therefore a problem to be corrected, or an appropriate reality for an ecclesial body that values freedom of conscience and dialogue around difficult contemporary issues. The chapter develops a line of argument rooted in the study's qualitative interviews that ecclesial openness, which is affirmed in the qualitative interviews with study participants, is possible only within a context of the church's serious commitment to making disciples of its members. Finally, the study draws out some of the implications of the practical-theological dialogue, which generates a few concrete suggestions which can guide the church in meeting the challenges presented and in continuing to wrestle with the moral questions of war and violence.

3

Literature Review

OVERVIEW

THE LITERATURE REVIEW FOCUSES on scholarship by key authors whose work serves to justify and frame the identified central questions and to provide the base upon which the study rests. The first section situates nonviolence within a wider ethical literature in order to distinguish this response to war and violence and also to show that nonviolence is not a clean alternative to just war theory, as is commonly believed. Just war theory is a specific response to the problem of war while nonviolence is connected to a wider lifestyle; therefore the assumption that just war and nonviolence can or should be easily compared and contrasted is a false assumption. It will be shown that nonviolence must be defined and understood on its own terms if it is to be appreciated as a valid and compelling approach to the ethical problem of war and violence. This section takes a closer look at the differences between just war and nonviolence in order to delineate some of the major nuances between them.

The second section delves more specifically into theologies of nonviolence. Included are Methodist authors as well as other key scholars on the subject of nonviolence. This part of the review introduces the range of theological bases for Christian nonviolence and discusses some of the arguments and issues involved. Here it will be shown that although theologies of nonviolence abound, few focus on how such a commitment plays out concretely in the lives of nonviolent persons and communities. For the most part, theologies of nonviolence follow an applied model which begins with theological norms and principles and then moves to prescriptions for Christian theology and ethics.

The third section of the review develops an understanding of "lived theology" as an approach which is complementary to but provides deeper analysis than the applied models noted in the second section. This practical-theological approach seeks to understand the commitment to nonviolence as it is maintained by beliefs and concrete practices within the real-life contexts of people whose lives and work reflect the commitment to nonviolence. A lived theology approach assumes the significance of practices (in this case, as they relate to the commitment to nonviolence) and recognizes the mutual exchange between practices and beliefs in shaping and informing one another.

The fourth section of the review draws out a conversation among Methodist scholars which raises serious questions related to pluralism within a church's doctrine. This section also hints at the confusion that may arise from doctrinal pluralism by highlighting the differing views of Methodist scholars regarding what the church actually teaches about war, peace, and nonviolence. Taken together, these four sections provide the background materials and information needed to frame and address the central questions posed by this study.

DISTINGUISHING POSITIONS: NONVIOLENCE AND THE JUST WAR TRADITION

In order to understand contemporary commitments to nonviolence, it is first important to name the alternative which proponents of nonviolence reject—the just war tradition, which has been called "the dominant framework for the analysis of the morality of war."[1] The sheer volume of social ethical reflection on just war is overwhelming; therefore this section of the literature review is purposefully limited in scope. A brief review of several key authors will serve to locate nonviolence in relation to the just war tradition and to delineate basic differences. Referencing some of the scholarship on nonviolence and just war, this part of the review argues that nonviolence and the just war tradition, despite sharing some common presumptions or values, are in fact very different responses to the moral dilemma of war and violence. Consequently, conversation between these two responses reveals important questions for continued ethical deliberation about how the church responds to these and related moral issues.

1. Shannon, *War or Peace?*, xi.

A helpful point of departure for such discussion is *The Westminster Dictionary of Christian Ethics*, in which James Turner Johnson names just war tradition as the positive answer to the question, "May a Christian ever justifiably take part in violence?"[2] Nonviolence is described as the negative answer to the question and is considered to be "a major strand alongside just war tradition in Christian attitudes toward war."[3] Early developments of the just war tradition occurred in a historical context in which the church and the state were closely related and in which the Roman Empire, suddenly a Christian state, had to be defended from invasion. Throughout different historical periods the just war tradition has been further developed into what is now understood as the criteria for justifiable resort for involvement in a war and justifiable means of engaging in a war.[4]

Joseph Allen's introductory work, *War: A Primer for Christians*, offers a straightforward explanation of the two positions and notes a few of the major differences. In taking up the pacifist standpoint, Allen distinguishes between the "pragmatic," which argues that nonviolence works effectively,[5] and the "witnessing" argument which would say that war is "incompatible" with what it means to follow Jesus.[6] While pragmatic pacifism tries to think creatively about ways to make political change and also "reminds us of the great cost of violence,"[7] it does not always take seriously the "depth and stubbornness of human sin" and can often exaggerate the effectiveness of nonviolent resistance.[8] While witnessing pacifism sees the theological basis of the pacifist stance and takes very seriously the

---

2. Johnson, "Just War," 328.

3. Ibid.

4. Ibid. It is not my intention to give a full account of the classical just war criteria, as this has been sufficiently accomplished on numerous occasions. For further explanation of the criteria, see: Joseph Fahey, "Conscience and War," in Fahey and Armstrong, *A Peace Reader*, 80–85; Joseph L. Allen, "Just-War Thinking," in Allen, *War: A Primer for Christians*, 31–52; United States Catholic Bishops, *Challenge of Peace: God's Promise and Our Response*; Ramsey, *The Just War: Force and Political Responsibility*; and Childress, "Just-War Criteria."

5. Allen, *War*, 20.

6. Ibid., 21.

7. Ibid., 24.

8. Ibid., 25.

idea of Christian discipleship,[9] Allen wonders if using violence to prevent violence against others is not, in some instances, the loving thing to do.[10]

Turning to the just war standpoint, Allen delineates the just war criteria of justifiable resort (justifiable cause, legitimate authority, last resort, declaration of war aims, proportionality, reasonable chance of success, and right intention) and justifiable means (principle of discrimination and proportionality). According to Allen, the strength of the just war approach is its realism about the reality of conflicts among people and nations[11] and its greater willingness to grapple with the complexities of violence and restraint against sin.[12] Criticisms of this approach include whether it too often simply justifies whatever a government wishes to do,[13] whether there can be a justifiable war given today's technological and weapons advances,[14] and questions about the adequacy of the just war criteria themselves.[15]

Among the scholarship attempting to describe and distinguish between just war and nonviolence, various interpretations exist about the differences between the two. James Finn asserts that each position begins with mainly pacifist assumptions – that peace is a primary value of a "high order" as opposed to the evil that is war, and that common humanity among people rails against the notion of the use of violent means to address conflicts. "But from there they diverge. The pacifist position states that the use of force to fend off or to overcome an evil is incompatible with the gospel. The other position states that some evils are so great and so threatening that the presumption against violence must be overridden; war under those conditions may be justifiable."[16]

J. Bryan Hehir distinguishes between the two positions in his "assessment of whether the divergent conclusions of pacifism and the just-war ethic are rooted in some shared moral vision."[17] For Hehir, the two share convictions about the sanctity of human life and the ensuing conviction

9. Ibid., 27.
10. Ibid., 28.
11. Ibid., 47.
12. Ibid., 48.
13. Ibid.
14. Ibid., 50.
15. Idib., 51.
16. Finn, "Pacifism and Justifiable War," 3.
17. Hehir, "Just-War Ethic," 24.

against taking that life. They agree that war is always a moral problem. However the two positions take different paths when the question of force as a tool for the provision of justice arises in concrete settings of conflict.

> The pacifist moral conviction about the inviolability of human life is so absolute, and the pacifist religious belief about the ministry and message of Jesus is so tied to a nonviolent meaning, that no conflict of values, even the defense of innocent life, can legitimize overriding the presumption.... Briefly, the pacifist ethic has a single rule and it is absolute: force is never to be used; it is incompatible with the Christian vocation. The just-war ethic has a multiplicity of rules; it begins with the pacifist presumption, but it acknowledges the possibility of the presumption yielding to a rule-governed use of force, shaped by a multiplicity of criteria. Common premises yield diverse conclusions. The journey from premise to conclusion is shaped not only by different patterns of moral reasoning, but also by positions on theological anthropology and diverse readings of the empirical data of history.[18]

In *Love Your Enemies: Discipleship, Pacifism, and Just War Theory*, ethicist Lisa Cahill provides somewhat deeper analysis of the differences, ultimately deciding that just war and pacifism cannot be considered two sides of the same coin. Cahill begins her treatment of pacifism and just war with the assertion that "they are both generally agreed to arise out of a common concern to avoid violence."[19] The major differences, however, greatly outweigh the few commonalities. While both pacifists and just war advocates of a Christian persuasion see the Scriptures as foundational to their understandings of how Christians should respond to war and violence,[20] different understandings of biblical teachings lead to conflicting conclusions about how Christians are to respond. Cahill notes that those who emphasize the "inbreaking presence of the kingdom" are usually "pacifists in their dedication to kingdom faithfulness."[21] Those who would fall into the just war camp "do not deny the New Testament mandate to disciples to live a transformed life, but they give that mandate less practical force through a process of translation that gives great weight to the

18. Ibid., 24–25.
19. Cahill, *Love Your Enemies*, 1.
20. Ibid., 9.
21. Ibid., 12.

social context and more freedom to the biblical and ethical interpreter."[22]
While similarity exists between pacifist and just war acknowledgements
that the life, work, and teachings of Jesus call the Christian disciple to
nonviolence and peace, the issue that divides is *"how* the mandate to live
in love, peace, and forgiveness is to function in the practical moral life."[23]
To unpack this issue, Cahill asks: "Is [the mandate] an absolute principle
or even rule, binding in a clear and specific way each and every decision a
Christian may face in which violent action is a possible outcome? Is it an
ideal, which encourages us onward, but to whose distance in this life we
must be resigned?"[24]

Finally, argues Cahill, the most crucial distinction between pacifism
and just war theory is "the realization that [pacifism] is above all not a
theory but a communal practice in imitation of Christ's servanthood and
cross."[25] Pacifism more than just war thinking "is embedded in a concrete,
shared, and converted way of life."[26] Ultimately, "Christian pacifism is
nourished primarily in spiritual fellowship, prayer, and communal reded-
ication to social action; just war theory is refined through more analytical
means, by increasingly stringent and self-critical application of its criteria,
increasingly nuanced to changing historical and technological contexts
of war."[27] While just war theory attempts to limit the circumstances and
the manner in which violence might be deemed appropriate or necessary,
pacifism is less about "an ethical reply to the violence question" and more
about a lifestyle or "practical embodiment" of religious faith.[28]

No literature review on the conversation between nonviolence and
the just war tradition—particularly for a study on United Methodism—
would be complete without inclusion of the work of Paul Ramsey. Ramsey
is not only a leading scholar-advocate of the just war tradition but is also a
Methodist. Ramsey does not share with Cahill the view that just war and
nonviolence are similar in their presumption against violence, or at least
he goes further to describe the degree to which each eschews violence.

22. Ibid.

23. Ibid., 13.

24. Ibid.

25. Ibid., 235.

26. Ibid.

27. Ibid.

28. Ibid., 2.

Ramsey contends that the two "do not share an equivalent rejection of violence."[29] Pacifism assumes the priority of peace, while just war assumes the priority of justice. As he describes it, "Just cause is overarching in just-war theory; within that, last resort comes into play. . . . Thus a presumption against injustice is a lexically prior presumption to the 'presumption against going to war' under 'last resort.' Confusion, not clarity, comes from saying that this is like pacifism's rejection of any use of violent means."[30]

Similar to Cahill's assertion above regarding the "crucial difference" between just war and nonviolence, in a chapter entitled "Can a Pacifist Tell a Just War?" Ramsey makes it very clear that just war is a theory of statecraft: "In all that I have ever written on the morality of war I have been quite consciously drawing upon a wider theory of statecraft and of political justice."[31] Given this, Ramsey questions the validity of pacifist attempts to discredit the just war tradition since the pacifist has "abdicated from the beginning the task of searching out the true meaning of the just war theory and the requirements this imposes upon us under the conditions of modern war."[32] To undergird his assertion that just war doctrine is precisely a theory of statecraft, Ramsey explains the adoption of just war thinking in connection with the Christianization of the state under Constantine:

> The change-over to just-war doctrine and practice was not a "fall" from the original purity of Christian ethics; but, however striking a turning-full-circle, this was a change of tactics only. The basic strategy remained the same: responsible love and service of one's neighbors in the texture of the common life. The primary motive and foundation for now approving Christian participation in warfare was the same as that which before, in a different social context, led Christians out of Christlike love for neighbor wholly to disapprove of the use of armed force. Christians simply came to see that the service of the real needs of all the men for whom Christ died required more than personal, witnessing action. It also

29. Ramsey, *Speak Up for Just War or Pacifism*, 54.

30. Ibid., 54.

31. Ibid., 260.

32. Ibid., 259. One could make the opposite argument as well: that attempts by just war advocates to discredit nonviolence are equally nonsensical since the just war advocate has denounced the "true meaning" of the nonviolent lifestyle "and the requirements this imposes" upon those who, in faith, make that commitment.

required them to be involved in maintaining the organized social
and political life in which all men live.[33]

In short, it is radically different views of church-state relations which undergird commitments to nonviolence and to the just-war tradition.

This assertion is further described in the writing of Stanley Hauerwas who, like Ramsey, sees fundamental incompatibilities between the just war tradition and nonviolence. Citing Ramsey's view of just war as a political strategy, Hauerwas reminds critics of nonviolence that they wrongly assume that pacifism can be neatly dismissed as an alternative to war. For Hauerwas the problem lies in presenting pacifism "as if it were an alternative to just war—that is, as a principled position that is meant to determine the policy of states. As I have tried to show, that is simply not how Christian pacifism, when it is Christologically and eschatologically determined, works."[34] Christian pacifism is "not so much a 'position' as a way of life in community";[35] because nonviolence is not just a political strategy, Hauerwas can only disagree with Ramsey's assertion that "nonviolence as a political strategy is war by another means."[36] As Hauerwas states elsewhere, "Christian nonviolence, in short, does not begin with a theory or conception about violence, war, 'the state or society,' and so on, but rather with practices such as forgiveness and reconciliation."[37]

A few important questions arise from this dialogue between nonviolence and just war. For example, is there a particular ecclesiological stance or preference that coincides with each of the two positions? Can the two be held simultaneously by an individual or a community? Where does the mandate of neighbor love come into play? Is justice for the neighbor a gospel value, and if so, what is its role in both just war and nonviolence? These questions are noted here as important points of contact for practical-theological reflection in chapter 6.

CHRISTIAN THEOLOGIES OF NONVIOLENCE

Having argued that nonviolence and just war cannot be compared neatly as opposite approaches to the problem of war and violence, this chapter

33. Ramsey, *War and the Christian Conscience*, xvii.
34. Hauerwas, "Epilogue: A Pacifist Response to the Bishops," 164.
35. Ibid., 164.
36. Ibid., 178.
37. "Can a Pacifist Think about War?" in Hauerwas, *Dispatches from the Front*, 130.

turns now to a more in-depth review of literature on nonviolence itself. As an investigation into the lived theology of nonviolence, this study requires a review of scholarship on Christian conceptions of nonviolence. This section of the review provides a survey of the range of theological bases for nonviolence, demonstrating that there is no single and coherent nonviolent position or posture. The section also provides a framework for practical-theological reflection in later chapters, which will deal with the principles and practices of nonviolence as they are identified by individuals who are attempting to live out of a commitment to nonviolence. Importantly, the review will demonstrate the lack of scholarship on nonviolence as it is actually lived and practiced in the daily lives of those who claim it as central to Christian faith. While a few scholars make some reference to "practices" in their theologies of nonviolence, the scholarship summarized below mostly follows an applied-theology model.

One prolific author-theologian is the Methodist Walter Wink, whose book *The Powers That Be: Theology for a New Millennium* seeks to dispel the myth of "redemptive violence" and focuses on Christological foundations in his theology of nonviolence. Wink emphasizes the radicality of Jesus' life and teachings and laments the early church's willingness to downplay that radicality as the church and the state began to align.[38] Christianity's "accommodation to power politics through the infinitely malleable ideology of the just war, its abandonment of the Christus Victor theory of the atonement for the blood theory, its projection of the reign of God into an afterlife or the remote future—all this gutted the church's message of its most radical elements."[39] In Wink's view, Jesus offers a "third way" which is not "submission nor assault, flight nor fight" but a way which keeps open the potential for the "enemy" to renounce his own evil and wrongdoing.[40] For Wink, such nonviolence is "not a matter of legalism but of discipleship" because it lies at the heart of the gospel.[41] In addition, Wink argues that the potential for "practical nonviolence" to overcome systems of violence and oppression is untapped due to limited experience and primitive knowledge.[42] While his work is critical to an understanding

38. Wink, *Powers That Be*, 81.
39. Ibid., 90–91.
40. Ibid., 110.
41. Ibid., 135.
42. Ibid., 112–13.

of some of the theological foundations of nonviolence, and despite his emphasis on *practical* nonviolence, Wink does not expressly discuss the ways in which nonviolence plays out and is practiced in the daily lives of those who maintain such a commitment.

John Howard Yoder's *The Politics of Jesus* also takes up the centrality of the biblical Jesus as the basis for an ethic of nonviolence. Yoder notes that the biblical Jesus is not considered normative for mainstream ethics;[43] decrying this state of affairs, he asserts that the very idea of the Incarnation means "that God broke through the borders of our standard definition of what is human and gave a new, formative definition in Jesus."[44] As the sole bearer of a "genuinely human existence,"[45] Jesus is "a model of radical political action"[46] and therefore cannot be ignored in any discussion of Christian nonviolence in the contemporary world. Particularly important for Yoder's theology of nonviolence is an emphasis on the community of Christ, the church, for "Christian social strategy."[47] For Yoder, "the church must be a sample of the kind of humanity within which, for example, economic and racial differences are surmounted. Only then will it have anything to say to the society that surrounds it about how those differences must be dealt with. Otherwise preaching to the world a standard of reconciliation which is not its own experience will be neither honest nor effective."[48]

Despite this more positive reference to the value of effectiveness, Yoder is clear in his critique of pacifist views that operate "on the level of means alone, as if the pacifist were making the claim that he can achieve what war promises to achieve, but do it just as well or even better without violence."[49] The most truly Christian pacifism is that which is "meaningful only if Christ be he who Christians claim him to be."[50] Such a pacifism is "one in which the calculating link between our obedience and ultimate

43. Yoder, *Politics of Jesus*, 4.
44. Ibid., 99.
45. Ibid., 145.
46. Ibid., 2.
47. Ibid., 149.
48. Ibid., 150–51.
49. Ibid., 239.
50. Ibid., 237.

efficacy has been broken, since the triumph of God comes through resurrection and not through effective sovereignty or assured survival."[51]

Yoder's commitment to a Jesus-centered pacifism appears again in his book *Nevertheless: Varieties of Religious Pacifism*, where he delineates twenty-nine distinguishable arguments against the violence of war. For Yoder, the pacifist stance "is not just one specific position, spoken for authoritatively ... [but] is a wide gamut of views that vary and are sometimes even contradictory."[52] Amid these twenty-nine views, Yoder claims the "Pacifism of the Messianic Community" as the only position that "collapses if Jesus be not Christ or if Jesus Christ be not Lord."[53] This book is an important typology for recognizing that the terms "nonviolence" and "pacifism" actually cover a wide range of views and cannot be simplistically boiled down into one position. Notable for the aims of this dissertation, however, is the absence of any discussion of practices of nonviolence or a concept of lived theology among those who hold this commitment. The theological grounding of Yoder's theology of nonviolence is clear, but how that theology might play out concretely in the lives of those who would subscribe to this theological grounding is left unstudied.

Basing much of his own writing about nonviolence on Yoder's work is Stanley Hauerwas, who argues as well for the "ethical significance" of Jesus in his life, death, and resurrection and for how the Christian disciple lives over and above the importance of Christological claims about salvation.[54] It is the narrative of Jesus' life that teaches us how to "be like God" which we do by "following the teachings of Jesus and thus learning to be his disciples."[55] Like Yoder, Hauerwas sees Jesus' life as the embodiment of "a way of life that God has made possible here and now";[56] for Hauerwas, nonviolence is central to Jesus' way of life and therefore must be central to the Christian disciple's way of life.

Taking cues from Yoder, Hauerwas too challenges the church to be the church, for this is the community that helps people to "develop the

---

51. Ibid., 239.

52. Yoder, *Nevertheless*, 12.

53. Ibid., 137.

54. Hauerwas, *Peaceable Kingdom*, 72.

55. Ibid., 75.

56. Ibid., 82.

resources to stand within the world witnessing to the peaceable kingdom."[57] Because the church is a "foretaste" of the kingdom (though not the kingdom), it "must be a clear manifestation of a people who have learned to be at peace with themselves, one another, the stranger, and of course, most of all, God."[58] The Christian community which follows Jesus seriously recognizes that faithfulness is more important than effectiveness and therefore can never use unjust means in its pursuit of justice. Hauerwas is clear on this point: "the church is finally known by the character of the people who constitute it, and if we lack that character, the world rightly draws the conclusion that the God we worship is in fact a false God."[59]

As highlighted above, Hauerwas stakes a firm claim for the normativity of nonviolence in and for the church and does express some interest in the ways in which the very practices of nonviolence can move communities toward nonviolence. In *Dispatches from the Front*, Hauerwas argues that "any compelling account of Christian nonviolence requires the display of practices of a community that has learned to embody nonviolence in its everyday practices."[60] In an endnote related to this statement, he further argues that "even to know what constitutes violence and/or war, one already must have been made part of practices that are nonviolent. What must be resisted are suggestions that 'we' all know what violence and/or war is abstracted from particular communities' histories."[61] Furthermore, Hauerwas asserts in *In Good Company: The Church as Polis*, that his "strategy is to try to help us recover the everyday practices that constitute that *polis* called church.... What we Christians have lost is just how radical our practices are, since they are meant to free us from the excitement of war and the lies so characteristic of this world."[62] For Hauerwas, the church is that "company" that has learned the practices and skills necessary to truthful worship—such "material habits" are what "make us what we are."[63] However, while Hauerwas emphasizes the need for theological convictions to be "practically embodied,"[64] he does not appear explicitly to draw

---

57. Hauerwas, "The Servant Community," 377.

58. Ibid., 372.

59. Ibid., 387.

60. Hauerwas, *Dispatches*, 117.

61. Ibid., 220.

62. Hauerwas, *In Good Company*, 8.

63. Ibid., 9.

64. Hauerwas, *Dispatches*, 3.

out how nonviolence can or should be practically embodied in the lives of those United Methodists who do make such a commitment.

Moving toward further Christological reflection, Ron Sider stakes a claim for principled nonviolence in *Christ and Violence*, where he argues for the centrality of nonviolence to Jesus' life and teachings but places special emphasis on Jesus' death as a "vicarious death for the sake of others"[65] which is the "very heart of our commitment to nonviolence."[66] The atonement, according to Sider, reveals to us the manner by which God reconciles God's enemies; therefore "any rejection of the nonviolent way in human relations involves a heretical doctrine of the atonement."[67] Here Sider's work reflects an applied-theology approach, in which he begins with theological principles (Christology and atonement theology) and then makes a claim for the normativity of Christian nonviolence. In *Non-Violence: The Invincible Weapon?*, Sider moves to a more practical view by highlighting a variety of cases and contexts in which nonviolence has been an effective tool for political and social change. These examples of success cause Sider to claim that "what exists is possible"[68] and that what is needed is serious exploration of nonviolence as a realistic option.[69] While Sider here emphasizes a more practical approach to nonviolence, there is no attempt to look at the lived theology of nonviolence as it is *practiced* in the lives of those who consider themselves to be nonviolent.

J. Denny Weaver also takes up the subject of atonement theology and nonviolence in his expansive work, *The Nonviolent Atonement*. Atonement theology, according to Weaver, starts with the violent killing of Jesus, out of which "something good happened, namely the salvation of sinners."[70] Weaver believes that current atonement theology is based on a retributive model of criminal justice, whereby justice is reached by exacting punishment.[71] Furthermore, utilizing the critiques leveled by black, feminist, and womanist theologies against current atonement theology, Weaver shows how these "contextual theologies"[72] have challenged "earlier theological

65. Sider, *Christ and Violence*, 33.

66. Ibid., 33–34.

67. Ibid., 34.

68. Sider, *Non-Violence*, 7.

69. Ibid., 83.

70. Weaver, *Nonviolent Atonement*, 2.

71. Ibid.

72. Ibid., 4.

efforts to justify violence or oppression of women and people of color by appeal to the suffering of Jesus or the submission of Jesus to suffering required by a divine mandate."[73] Weaver rejects the prevailing atonement theories (Christus Victor, Satisfaction, and Moral Influence models) and replaces them with what he calls "Narrative Christus Victor." As Weaver develops it, this model sees the object of Jesus' death as the powers of evil;[74] what Jesus' death "accomplishes" is not the salvation of sinners but the witness of the reign of God through defeat of the power of evil in the world. Rather than passive standers-by, humans are actively involved in their salvation; when a person is saved, "she changes loyalty from the rule of evil to the reign of God by accepting the call of God to new life in the reign of God. It is not a mere change of legal status before God, but a change in character and allegiance that means nothing—in fact, has not occurred—if there is no life lived according to the reign of God."[75]   For Weaver, "the nonviolent character of the ethics of the reign of God is of particular significance."[76] Weaver's work—perhaps more than any other theology of nonviolence discussed in this part of the literature review— might be considered an example of practical-theological reflection in that it brings the "contextual theologies" of black, feminist, and womanist authors into critical dialogue with classical atonement theology.

Two theologians take issue with Weaver's critical re-thinking of atonement theology. In his essay "The Gospel of Peace and the Violence of God," Scott Holland emphasizes the concept of God as "wholly other," which places a limit on "all ethical, theological, or political doctrines or dogmas."[77] With reference to Luther's theology of the "hidden and revealed God," Holland suggests that even in revelation and incarnation, "there is something of the transcendent God that remains hidden."[78] To assume otherwise can lead us to make God in our own image. Holland's work in the Nigerian context, where horrific violence is a common experience for many, leads him to challenge the notion of a God who is absolutely and necessarily nonviolent. He argues that "linking the gospel

---

73. Ibid., 5.

74. Ibid., 70.

75. Ibid., 79–80.

76. Ibid., 80.

77. Holland, "Gospel of Peace and the Violence of God," 139.

78. Ibid., 138.

of peace to a notion of the benevolence of nature and the pacifism of God, as some contemporary peace church theologians are tempted to do, is unthinkable and unbelievable to most Nigerian pastors and theologians."[79] For people who have witnessed such violence, it is precisely the belief that God is a God of justice who does, in the end, exact judgment from those who have committed such atrocities that creates the space to live nonviolently in the present. Holland asks whether it is possible "that a theopoetic acknowledgement of the violence of Hidden God might indeed transform the aggressive energies in the human psyche, soul, and body into active and nonviolent expressions of peacemaking on earth."[80] More pointedly, "could it be that because Yahweh is a warrior, we can be a people of peace?"[81]

This line of thinking is echoed by Miroslav Volf in *Exclusion and Embrace: A Theological Exploration of Identity, Otherness, and Reconciliation*. While the cross teaches us that there is only one alternative in the face of violence—that of nonviolent and selfless love—we must make sense of images of God's violence, particularly in Biblical apocalyptic literature where God deals with injustice so violently. Volf argues for the erroneousness of the assumption of correlation between "divine action and human behavior."[82] After all, "humans are not God. There is a duty prior to the duty of imitating God, and that is the duty *of not wanting to be God*, of letting God be God and humans be humans.... Preserving the fundamental difference between God and nonGod, the biblical tradition insists that there are things which only God may do. One of them is to use violence."[83] It is precisely the belief in God's justice at history's end which creates the space for us to live nonviolently now. For Volf, belief in a divine justice is a requirement of authentic nonviolent living.[84]

In the theologies that remain to be noted in this section, an applied model generally dominates although there are occasional hints of a more practical-theological approach. In *Blessed Are the Peacemakers: A Christian Spirituality of Nonviolence*, Michael Battle posits a Trinitarian foundation

79. Ibid.

80. Ibid., 142.

81. Ibid., 144.

82. Volf, *Exclusion and Embrace*, 301.

83. Ibid.

84. Ibid., 304.

for nonviolence, arguing that "Christian spirituality seen through the image of God's Trinity addresses personal spirituality only to the extent that it enables communal practices of nonviolence."[85] Peacemaking is to be understood as the "flourishing of God's triune image of community" throughout creation.[86] He defines Christian spirituality as "nonviolent lifestyle";[87] "at the heart of Christian spirituality . . . is the practice of nonviolence in which Jesus demonstrated the ultimate effect of nonviolence through resurrection."[88] It is this lifestyle, grounded in and dependent upon the Triune God, which serves to redeem creation.[89] Battle suggests that two traditions of spiritual direction, discernment and communal process, can be particularly helpful to the goal of "peacemaking as spiritual direction toward sainthood."[90] Battle's discussion of these spiritual disciplines as key to the development and sustenance of the nonviolent lifestyle—as part of his larger discussion of nonviolence as crucial to Christian formation—is particularly insightful to the present study. While he does not explicitly discuss a lived theology of nonviolence, Battle's work appears to be one of the few examples of scholarship that intentionally moves into the realm of actual *practices* of nonviolence.

The New Testament scholar Richard Hays calls for the normativity of nonviolence based on his reading of the New Testament texts. In *The Moral Vision of the New Testament: A Contemporary Introduction to New Testament Ethics*, Hays' exegetical work on Matthew 5:38–48 leads him to conclude that "the passage teaches a norm of nonviolent love of enemies."[91] Hays focuses on this passage from the Sermon on the Mount because it is often viewed as the "clearest call for Jesus' disciples to forsake violence"[92] but then tests this passage against the rest of the New Testament writings. Based on his reading of all four Gospels, Acts, the Pauline corpus, Hebrews and the Epistles, and Revelation, Hays concludes that the "testimony of the New Testament writers" on the issue of nonviolence is "impressively

85. Battle, *Blessed Are the Peacemakers*, 4.
86. Ibid., 34.
87. Ibid., 2.
88. Ibid., 195.
89. Ibid., 29.
90. Ibid., 194.
91. Hays, *Moral Vision of the New Testament*, 329.
92. Ibid., 319.

univocal."[93] Careful to cover all bases, Hays attends to passages that would seem to justify violence (Matthew 10:34, Luke 22:36, and the cleansing of the Temple) but concludes that, when framed properly within the text, these cannot serve as warrants for violence.[94] Ultimately, judges Hays, if one "were seeking to identify the ethical matters at the heart of Christian discipleship as spotlighted by the New Testament,"[95] one would surely determine nonviolence to be one of those matters. Hays' intention is not to discuss how nonviolence is lived out but to provide Biblical-theological rationale for the normativity of Christian pacifism.

This section of the literature review reveals that there is a wide variety of sources and rationales for Christian conceptions of nonviolence; these sources serve as an important foundation for understanding the theological sources of nonviolence as they are identified by interviewees in the qualitative part of this investigation. One key commonality among the theologies of nonviolence reviewed here is that most exhibit what can be called an *applied* theology of nonviolence. Each theology begins with one or more areas of theological normativity—Christology (especially Wink, Yoder, and Hauerwas), conceptions of the nature of God (Weaver, Volf, and Holland), Scripture (Hays most explicitly), ecclesiology (Yoder, Hauerwas), and any degree or combination of these—and moves from there to a call for the normativity of Christian nonviolence. Admittedly the contributions by Hauerwas and Battle are somewhat unique in their discussions of practices of nonviolence: Hauerwas in calling for the embodiment of nonviolence in everyday practices of Christians and Battle in discussing specific practices of spiritual formation toward the nonviolent lifestyle. However, it remains that both advance their theologies of nonviolence by starting with theological beliefs and assumptions. In addition, the works cited in this section by Weaver and Holland stand out as possible exceptions to an applied model because their theologies have been worked out in conjunction either with the critiques of those who have suffered violence (Weaver with black, womanist, and feminist theologies) or within a specific context of violence (Holland in Nigeria).

The current project aligns more with these studies of nonviolence in that it investigates how those who have committed to this position

93. Ibid., 329.
94. Ibid., 332–35.
95. Ibid., 313.

understand the theories and practices involved in their commitments. In seeking to draw out the lived theology of nonviolence through interviews with nonviolent United Methodist Christians, this study moves beyond a more theory-based model of thinking about nonviolence. While the study recognizes the contribution of those models, especially for drawing out key theological sources of Christian nonviolence, it moves toward deeper analysis by exploring how such theories are lived out and displayed through concrete practices that guide, shape, and constitute the commitment to nonviolence and how beliefs and practices of "regular people" might challenge and enrich church doctrine and teaching.

LIVED THEOLOGY

To move beyond the applied model demonstrated in so many theologies of nonviolence, an argument is made in the third section of the literature review for the importance of the "lived theology" of nonviolence among contemporary United Methodist Christians and its contribution to dialogue with a doctrinal tradition that is judged to be pluralistic and therefore rather confusing. Exploration of this lived theology is a unique contribution of the dissertation. Scholarship that contributes to an understanding of lived theology is reviewed here, as are works that demonstrate the appropriateness of a study in lived theology for United Methodism. A working definition of how lived theology is conceived for the purposes of this study is offered at the conclusion to this section.

Guidance for the task of examining the lived theology of nonviolent United Methodists is given in *Lived Religion in America: Toward a History of Practice*, edited by David Hall. In his introduction to the book, Hall describes the project on lived religion as one that emphasizes the "daily life" of people and seeks to "encourage reflection on 'practice' as the center or focus of the Christian life."[96] "Practice" however is not confined simply to what people do but includes "the tensions, the ongoing struggle of definition, which are constituted within every religious tradition and that are always present in how people choose to act."[97] Furthermore, in his chapter "Everyday Miracles: The Study of Lived Religion," Robert Orsi suggests that the phrase "lived religion" connotes a sense that a person's daily life both shapes and tests religious meanings and convictions. As such, lived

96. Hall, "Introduction" in *Lived Religion in America*, vii.
97. Ibid., xi.

religion is "concerned with what people *do* with religious practice, and what they make with it of themselves and their worlds," thereby seeking "a more dynamic integration of religion and experience."[98]

The recent work by Dawne Moon on *God, Sex, and Politics: Homosexuality and Everyday Theologies* also informs the project's emphasis on lived theology. Moon argues that an understanding of "everyday theologies" challenges the assumption that people simply believe what their church doctrines say—an assumption which does not allow room for the idea that people have an "ability and mandate to learn and grow in faith."[99] Moreover, Moon argues that the theologies people hold develop not only from worship or reading Scripture but are founded also upon other influential texts, experiences, and relationships as people negotiate their way through the activities of daily life.[100] Scrutiny of everyday theologies (or lived theology, as the term is used in the current study) provides a range of the foundations undergirding why people believe what they believe and engage in the practices in which they engage. While Moon's study is conducted around issues of homosexuality, her insights, discovered through the lens of everyday theologies, inspire the current project's emphasis on discovering the lived theologies of nonviolent people.

In the Foreword to *Everyday Religion: Observing Modern Religious Lives*, edited by Nancy Ammerman, Peter Berger notes that while religious institutions play an important role in society, "much of religious life takes place outside these institutional locales. To limit the study of religion to these locales would be like, say, studying politics by only looking at the activities of organized political parties."[101] Ammerman, too, asserts the importance of understanding the richness of "everyday" religious activity: "Similarly, everyday implies the activity that happens outside organized religious events and institutions, but that does not mean that we discount the influence those institutions wield or that we neglect what happens within organized religion 'every day.' We are interested in all the ways in which nonexperts experience religion."[102] This kind of thinking definitely informs the current study and underscores one of its underly-

---

98. Orsi, "Everyday Miracles," 7–8.

99. Moon, *God, Sex, and Politics*, 13.

100. Ibid., 13–14.

101. Berger, "Foreword," v.

102. Ammerman, "Introduction," 5.

ing assumptions—namely, that United Methodists who decide to adopt a nonviolent ethic and lifestyle do so based *at least in part* on influences, experiences, and formation external to their own tradition, which does not view nonviolence as necessary to Christian faith and discipleship.

Sources that investigate practices and beliefs and the relationship between them inform the current project's emphasis on these aspects of nonviolence. Craig Dykstra's *Growing in the Life of Faith: Education and Christian Practices* argues that people "live into" faith and grow in faith by participating in the practices of the Christian community. As people learn such practices, those practices become part of the lives of those who participate in them; "increasingly, we come to live into them until they live in us."[103] The book *Practicing Theology: Beliefs and Practices in Christian Life*, edited by Miroslav Volf and Dorothy C. Bass, also informs this study's discussion of the interconnectedness of theory and practice. Bass suggests that an approach to theology based on the study of practices "provides a way of thinking about the close relation between thinking and doing."[104] Bass concisely states the relationship between beliefs and practices in her definition of Christian practices: "Christian practices are patterns of cooperative human activity in and through which life together takes shape over time in response to and in the light of God as known in Jesus Christ. Focusing on practices invites theological reflection on the ordinary, concrete activities of actual people—and also on the knowledge of God that shapes, infuses, and arises from these activities."[105]

The endeavor of this study to delve into the lived theology of nonviolence is conducive to a study focused on the United Methodist Church. Scott Jones writes that "the goal of United Methodist doctrine is a life of Christian discipleship."[106] As such, doctrine is always shaped by practice and vice versa. In fact all theology is practical in that it "answers questions arising out of Christian practice and should inform that practice by helping it better achieve its goals. There is thus a dialectical relationship be-

103. Dykstra, *Growing in the Life of Faith*, 45.

104. Volf and Bass, *Practicing the Faith*, 2.

105. Ibid., 3.

106. Jones, *United Methodist Doctrine*, 61. Certainly I do not wish to imply that a study in lived theology is fitting for the United Methodist Church over and against or in comparison to other traditions. I am simply making the argument that, given the nature of Methodist history, polity, and ecclesiology, a lived theology approach makes sense for the United Methodist Church.

tween all of Christian theology (practical, historical, and systematic) and the practice of the Christian faith."[107] If practice matters for and shapes doctrine and teaching, then this study, as an investigation into the "every-day" practice of nonviolence in the lives of United Methodist Christians, is an important contribution for informing the witness of the church.

Precedence for drawing out and listening to the lived theology of United Methodists is provided by Virgil Wesley Sexton in *Listening to the Church: A Realistic Profile of Grass Roots Opinion.* While outdated (the book was published in 1971), the book pulls together the results of a denomination-wide survey that addressed areas of concern and priori-ties for the future of the church. In the attempt "to avoid a bureaucratic, handed-down answer" regarding the direction of the church, the opinions of laity and clergy from across the country were collected using various methods of data collection: brief surveys, more in-depth questionnaires, and hearings conducted in different parts of the country.[108] Sexton notes the risks in using such data for deciphering the way forward. The United Methodist Church is not a "consensus church" whose course is set by ma-jority opinion but is instead an ecclesial body that seeks to follow the gos-pel of Christ. On the other hand, "the Holy Spirit leads and challenges all in the church—not just top leadership—to mission. Responsibility to seek relevant involvement for a denomination rests upon all, not just a few. . . . Together, churchmen and churchwomen must weigh data on trends, issues, and church needs in the light of the purpose of the Christian church."[109] It is the aim of the current study to facilitate a similar conver-sation between authoritative tradition in the United Methodist Church and those who may be challenging that tradition by the manner in which they live their lives according to a nonviolent ethic.

Similar convictions expressed by Henry Knight and Don Saliers in *The Conversation Matters: Why United Methodists Should Talk with One Another* also stand as an encouragement for this project's emphasis on the importance of lived theology. For Knight and Saliers, United Methodists are called to speak and listen to each other in part "because we stand in a tradition that honors communal theological thinking. John Wesley in-

107. Ibid., 72.
108. Sexton, *Listening to the Church*, 14–15.
109. Ibid., 17–18.

sisted on this from the beginning of the Methodist movement."[110] Knight and Saliers argue for the "recovery of Christian conference" because "it allows us to really listen to and learn from positions different than our own."[111] By listening to voices from the nonviolent community within United Methodism, this project hopes to offer learning and insight to the wider church.

Based on the scholarship cited above, for the purposes of this study I define "lived theology" as the theological beliefs, principles, and practices which constitute and sustain the faith commitments of an individual or community. A lived theology of nonviolence, then, would include the theological beliefs, principles, and practices which constitute and sustain the commitments to Christian nonviolence in the life of an individual or community.

UNITED METHODIST DOCTRINE AND TEACHING: CONSISTENCY AND INTERPRETATION

Embedded in the central research questions explored by this project is the assumption that the United Methodist Church maintains a multiplicity of teachings about issues of war, peace, and nonviolence. This section of the literature review includes a discussion of doctrinal authority and the need for its clarity within United Methodism. The review cites scholars on both sides of the argument: those who argue that the United Methodist Church is a dynamic denomination that is ever-changing and re-forming itself and therefore is open to differing views, and those who argue that inconsistency within the formal doctrine and teaching of the church—particularly when dealing with important moral and social issues—is a significant problem. The specific doctrinal content of the two main written sources of Methodist doctrine and teaching, the *Book of Discipline* and the *Book of Resolutions*, will be treated separately and more thoroughly in chapter 4, where textual analysis of these authoritative sources reveals the multiple views contained within United Methodist doctrine and teaching. Finally, a brief foray into the differing interpretations of Methodist scholars regarding key doctrinal texts further demonstrates not only the multiplicity of teachings on war and peace but also hints at the confusion that may arise from that multiplicity. The critiques leveled by these au-

110. Knight and Saliers, *Conversation Matters*, 12.
111. Ibid., 81.

thors will be treated more fully in the textual analysis in chapter 4, and a discussion of whether this multiplicity is indicative of doctrinal inclusion or confusion will take place in chapter 6.

The Need for Consistency?

The question of consistency within authoritative Methodist doctrine becomes an important issue for this study.[112] On issues of doctrine and authority, writes Thomas Langford in *Doctrine and Theology in the United Methodist Church*, Methodism has had "a tradition which recognizes itself as open and freshly formative."[113] While contemporary Methodism is not void of continuity with past ways of being Methodist, it is a faith tradition which is "radically historical; that is, it is set within specific historical contexts and is affected by these settings."[114] Albert Outler too points to the pluralism of the United Methodist doctrinal standards, noting that such pluralism is not "a license to doctrinal recklessness or indifferentism" but "holds in dynamic balance both the biblical focus of all Christian doctrine and also the responsible freedom that all Christians must have in their theological reflections and public teaching."[115] For Outler, United Methodists view such theological pluralism "as a positive theological virtue."[116] While Langford and Outler both discuss theological pluralism in the United Methodist Church, neither identifies the plurality of views on social issues in particular, let alone the potential implications of such plurality.

While John Cobb, Jr. does not refer specifically to pluralism of views on social issues, he does point to the negative outcomes that theological pluralism can have. Cobb notes wording in the *Book of Discipline* which "affirms [the church's] openness to divergent theological traditions and projects" and which encourages diversity within United Methodist theol-

---

112. An interesting and insightful parallel study of Catholic documents and the existence of pluralism within the Catholic moral tradition on issues of just war and nonviolence is offered by J. Bryan Hehir, "The Just-War Ethic and Catholic Theology: Dynamics of Change and Continuity."

113. Langford, *Doctrine and Theology in the United Methodist Church*, 16.

114. Ibid., 13.

115. Outler, "Introduction to the Report of the 1968–72 Theological Study Commission," 21.

116. Ibid., 23.

ogy.[117] Noting the cost of such pluralism, Cobb points to the "theological indifferentism" and the confusion among United Methodists regarding what they are to believe about theological claims. In addition—and herein lie some of the implications of multiple views on major social issues— pluralism has led to a weakened sense of mission within Methodism. "Inevitably, the UMC turns in on itself to find its reason for existence and a basis for action. When it does so, many understandably seek unity of belief to replace the disappearing unity of purpose. Some of these individuals are disturbed to find the denomination's official statement so accepting of diversity."[118]

Scott Jones states the problem most clearly. In his view, contemporary ethical questions have caused a revival of interest in doctrine. People look to the teachings of their church as they grapple with difficult ethical problems. Jones argues that "the quality of [the church's] teaching has immense implications for all of its ministries. The quality of its social action and its ministries of social justice depend, at least in part, on the credibility, clarity, and cogency of its doctrine."[119] In seeming opposition to Albert Outler's claim that "doctrinal confusion cannot be overcome by official dogmatic pronouncement,"[120] Jones asserts that "unanswered questions" and teachings that are "unclear and vague" are "problematic if the Church really does believe its doctrine is important."[121] To address this problem, Jones suggests that the denomination must devote attention to the clarification of its doctrinal teaching, thereby strengthening the witness of the church.

Returning to the *Book of Discipline,* a clear and succinct statement of the need for consistency in United Methodist doctrine can be found within the pages of the church's "book of law" itself. After pointing to the long legacy of Methodist social concern and to "the connection between doctrine and ethics," the *Discipline* asserts: "a church lacking the courage to act decisively on personal and social issues loses its claim to moral authority."[122]

---

117. Cobb, "Is Theological Pluralism Dead in the U.M.C.?" 162.
118. Ibid., 163.
119. Jones, *United Methodist Doctrine,* 18.
120. Outler, "Introduction to the Report," 21.
121. Jones, *United Methodist Doctrine,* 57.
122. *Book of Discipline* (2004), 49.

Multiple Interpretations as Evidence of the Confusion

That the church has failed to speak and act "decisively" on the issue of war and nonviolence is demonstrated by the differing interpretations of church teaching that emerge from the writings of various Methodist scholars. Obvious confusion arises from current doctrine that specifically addresses the issue. A snapshot of these differing views is given here to support the claim that the official teaching of the United Methodist Church lacks clarity and leads to confusion within the church. The points raised by these authors form the foundation for practical-theological dialogue in chapter 6 between the doctrine and the lived theologies of nonviolent United Methodists. Expansion of these interpretations will appear in chapter 4, which provides a textual analysis of the actual content of the doctrinal statements around issues of war and nonviolence.

In a study entitled *This We Believe: The Articles of Religion and the Confession of Faith of the United Methodist Church*, Norman Madsen claims that these two documents, as part of the doctrinal standards of the church, "summarize the essence of the Christian faith."[123] Madsen interprets Article XVI of the Confession of Faith thus: "As the article indicates, although 'war and bloodshed are contrary to the gospel,' soldiering may be necessary. If our country and government are threatened, is not a Christian under the authority of the state responsible for the state's protection?"[124] In *Belief Matters: United Methodism's Doctrinal Standards*, Charles Yrigoyen encourages the reader to note "the strong statement that 'war and bloodshed' violate the Christian gospel."[125] Yrigoyen also insists that the Social Principles "are clear on the matter of war" but admits that the United Methodist Church is not a pacifist church.[126]

While Madsen and Yrigoyen see no claim for pacifism within Article XVI, D. Stephen Long argues precisely the opposite. In *Living the Discipline: United Methodist Theological Reflections on War, Civilization, and Holiness*, Long claims that the church is constitutionally a pacifist church and interprets Article XVI as the basis of that claim.[127] According

---

123. Madsen, *This We Believe*, 5.

124. Ibid., 88.

125. Yrigoyen, *Belief Matters*, 118.

126. Ibid.

127. Long, *Living the Discipline*, 1.

to Long, the United Methodist Church must reclaim its doctrinal heritage and, in so doing, will return to a pacifist commitment.

In *Dispatches from the Front: Theological Engagements with the Secular*, Stanley Hauerwas also cites Article XVI as an example of how the United Methodist Church posits itself against war. However, Hauerwas is quick to point to the inconsistency internal to United Methodist doctrinal teaching, revealed in later statements within the Social Principles that assert the church's support of people who choose to serve in the armed forces.[128]

In the forward to Herman Will's *A Will for Peace*, Bishop Leroy Hodapp, on the other hand, cites these same Social Principles as evidence of the church's "convictions" with regard to war.[129] Hodapp notes the pacifist-sounding statements in the Principles on "Military Service" and "War and Peace" as proof of the United Methodist emphasis on rejection of war but gives no indication of how statements that express the church's support for those who serve in the military should be interpreted and understood.

United Methodist theologian and just war advocate Paul Ramsey is particularly critical of the official teachings on war and nonviolence within church doctrine. In his discussion of the development of the Social Principles statement on "War and Peace," Ramsey concludes that the paragraph makes "sweeping pacifist statements" for the United Methodist Church.[130] If the church took the statement on "War and Peace" seriously, argues Ramsey, it would "mean that Methodist men and women should come out of the armed services and related industries."[131] However, Ramsey notes the inconsistency of the teaching by the fact that in the Social Principles statement on "Military Service," the church explicitly extends its support to people who choose to serve in the armed forces.[132]

This section of the review has raised issues related to the problems of pluralism and inconsistency and flags the key texts to be considered in the textual analysis of United Methodist doctrinal statements. In the following chapter, the actual content of the doctrinal tradition will be ex-

128. Hauerwas, *Dispatches*, 117.

129. Hodapp, "Foreword," vii.

130. Ramsey, *Speak Up*, 9.

131. Ibid., 8.

132. Ibid., 12.

amined in order to expose the plurality of views around issues of war and nonviolence and the study will wrestle with what it means for a church to hold within the limits of acceptability two differing responses to the moral problem of violence. While some authors have pointed to certain aspects of this inconsistency, the aim of this project is to analyze the texts more thoroughly in order to shed further light on the current state of doctrine and teaching on issues of war and nonviolence.

CONCLUSION

The scholarship reviewed in this chapter offers insight into nonviolence in and of itself as well as in relation to the more dominant approach of just war theory. The review lays the groundwork and rationale for textual analysis of current doctrine and teaching about war and nonviolence in authoritative United Methodist texts and provides the rationale for and description of "lived theology" as it will be used in this investigation. Finally, it also points to the appropriateness of a lived theology approach for a study in United Methodism and raises important questions of doctrinal plurality and consistency. These topics frame the central research questions that drive this project and will guide and support the research findings and practical-theological reflection in the following chapters.

4

A Pacifist Church or a Just War Church?

*Textual Analysis of Statements on War, Peace,
and Nonviolence in the* Book of Discipline
and the Book of Resolutions

THE PURPOSE OF THIS chapter is to demonstrate through textual analysis of United Methodism's official teachings that when it comes to questions of war and the use of violence, church doctrine contains a multiplicity of views which often seem to contradict one another. By tracing changes in the *Book of Discipline* and the *Book of Resolutions* and showing, where possible, how those changes and resolutions developed through the last several decades, the analysis will demonstrate that the official teaching of the United Methodist Church on matters of war and violence lacks clear definition. Interwoven throughout analysis of the texts is commentary, when available, by Methodist scholars who not only have offered their own positive or negative opinions on this multiplicity of views, but whose varying judgments about what the teachings mean serve as evidence of the doctrinal diversity of teachings on war and violence and help to raise the important questions that will be drawn out in the conclusion of this chapter. These questions include what it might mean for a church to hold in tandem conflicting views on major moral dilemmas and whether the doctrinal pluralism of views on war and violence should be judged as a confusion-causing problem or as an asset appropriate to the nature of Methodist ecclesiology. How the questions drive a lived theology approach—and how such an approach may inform the study and wrestle with these questions—will also be addressed at the conclusion.

THE *DISCIPLINE* ON WAR, PEACE, AND NONVIOLENCE: ARTICLE XVI AND THE SOCIAL PRINCIPLES

Article XVI

The United Methodist Church was born in 1968 at the Uniting Conference between the Methodist Church and the Evangelical United Brethren.[1] At the time of the 1968 union, the Methodist Church had as its governing statement the Articles of Religion while the Evangelical United Brethren (EUB) had the Confession of Faith. In the Plan of Union for what is now the United Methodist Church, "both [the Methodist Articles of Religion and the EUB Confession of Faith] were accepted as doctrinal standards for the new church."[2] The Articles of Religion and the Confession of Faith cover such important Christian doctrinal topics as the Holy Spirit, the church and worship, the Trinity, the Scriptures, original sin, justification, the sacraments, and other Christian themes. Included in the EUB Confession of Faith is Article XVI, which is entitled "Civil Government" and which states:

> We believe civil government derives its just powers from the sovereign God. As Christians we recognize the government under whose protection we reside and believe such governments should be based on, and be responsible for, the recognition of human rights under God. We believe war and bloodshed are contrary to the gospel and spirit of Christ. We believe it is the duty of Christian citizens to give moral strength and purpose to their respective governments through sober, righteous and godly living.[3]

This Article remains part of the "Doctrinal Standards and General Rules" of the United Methodist Church today.

D. Stephen Long has argued in *Living the Discipline: United Methodist Theological Reflections on War, Civilization, and Holiness* that the United Methodist Church is constitutionally a pacifist church even if it is not so largely in practice.[4] Long's argument is based primarily on Article XVI of the EUB Confession of Faith. Because Article XVI

---

1. *Book of Discipline* (2004), 9.

2. Ibid., 58. John Wesley's *Standard Sermons* and *Explanatory Notes upon the New Testament* were also included as doctrinal standards, although that fact is less important for our particular purposes.

3. *Book Discipline* (2004), 71.

4. Long, *Living the Discipline*, 1–2.

is part of the EUB Confession of Faith, and because the Confession of Faith remains part of the Doctrinal Standards of the current United Methodist Church, in technical terms at least, one could argue as Long does that Article XVI makes a normatively pacifist claim for the church in its statement that "we believe war and bloodshed are contrary to the gospel and spirit of Christ."

There is even more warrant for this claim if one takes into consideration the "Restrictive Rules" of the United Methodist constitution included in the *Book of Discipline*. The Restrictive Rules explicitly identify that which the General Conference may *not* do. These rules allow the General Conference to "have broad authority over the denomination except for those items protected by what are now called the Restrictive Rules."[5] Under Division Two (on organization), Section 3, Article 1, the constitution states that "the General Conference shall not revoke, alter, or change our Articles of Religion or establish any new standards or rules of doctrine contrary to our present existing and established standards of doctrine";[6] Article 2 states the same for the EUB Confession of Faith. This implies that not only is Article XVI of the Confession of Faith binding on the United Methodist Church, but the church can make no rule, policy, or doctrinal change that might "revoke, alter, or change" the Article.[7]

Even with the Restrictive Rules potentially working on his side, however, Long's argument is challenged by his jumping too quickly from the statements included in Article XVI to the claim that those statements call us to a "normatively pacifist" stance. Long claims that "the EUB had a relationship with the historic peace churches, and that relationship is reflected in Article XVI. This should lead us to consider seriously if we are not, in fact, by historical contingency and by the leading of the Holy Spirit, now fully within the realm of the historic peace churches."[8] However, he does not describe what this relationship is. It is true that Martin Boehm, one of the founders of the United Brethren in Christ Church (which would later merge with the Evangelical Church to form the EUB), was a Mennonite.[9]

5. Waltz, *Dictionary for United Methodists*, 161–62.

6. *Book of Discipline* (2004), 27.

7. Long does not make this observation himself; his case might have been strengthened had he chosen to include it in his claim that Article XVI claims pacifism for the United Methodist Church.

8. Long, *Living the Discipline*, 40.

9. Behney and Eller, *History of the Evangelical United Brethren Church*, 40.

But it is questionable whether this connection by "historical contingency" places the United Methodist Church "within the realm of the historic peace churches."

Long's claim is also challenged by the way in which the Evangelical United Brethren understood its own Article XVI prior to unification. Two years before the EUB was united to the Methodist Church to form the United Methodist Church, its bishops addressed the 1966 EUB General Conference in Chicago. Concerning the social problem of war, and referencing Article XVI in particular, the bishops stated that:

> With the possible exception of slavery, questions surrounding war have been the oldest social problems in the Christian church. Jesus is known as The Prince of Peace and early Christians refused to serve in the legions of the Caesars. However war-making and Christianity have had a long and constant affiliation. . . . Christians seemingly are unable to solve this controversial issue in a way which satisfies the consciences of all concerned. The EUB Confession of Faith, Article XVI, Civil Government, says: "We believe war and bloodshed are contrary to the gospel and spirit of Christianity." This is a very positive statement against war, yet conscientious objectors and active crusaders for peace are not too numerous in our denomination.[10]

While the bishops of the Evangelical United Brethren recognized the sentence in Article XVI to be a clear statement against war, they also admitted that pacifism was not understood in the EUB as a primary identifying characteristic of EUB members, clergy, or leadership.

Prior to this, a commentary by an EUB board refers to Article XVI as an "indictment against war,"[11] adding that "war deserves this isolation and prominence because it is the mother of a vile brood of many evils. It is a compounding of offenses against the 'gospel and spirit of Christ.'"[12] While arguing that this "Statement of Faith rests on the principle that it is contrary to Christian idealism," in the next breath any overwhelming identity of the Evangelical United Brethren with pacifism is negated by the statement that the "individual Christian must make the agoniz-

10. Board of Bishops, Evangelical United Brethren Church, *Episcopal Message to the General Conference*, 11–12.

11. Board of Christian Education and the Board of Evangelism, Evangelical United Brethren Church, *This We Believe*, 97.

12. Ibid., 98.

ing choice as to where duty and justice point him in a specific engagement and how much blood shall stain his hand or soul in the common defense."[13] The conclusion one might draw from this information is that if the Evangelical United Brethren itself did not understand Article XVI as calling the church to nonviolence, then there may be little plausibility in claiming that article as the source of Methodist claims of nonviolence.

Other Methodist scholars as well have offered interpretations of Article XVI, and the variety in those interpretations is indicative of the fact that this brief but important statement may not provide as clear a claim for pacifism as Long argues. As noted previously in chapter 3, Norman Madsen interprets Article XVI of the Confession of Faith thus: "As the article indicates, although 'war and bloodshed are contrary to the gospel,' soldiering may be necessary. If our country and government are threatened, is not a Christian under the authority of the state responsible for the state's protection?"[14] Charles Yrigoyen notes "the strong statement that 'war and bloodshed' violate the Christian gospel"[15]—and also insists that the Social Principles "are clear on the matter of war"—but admits that the United Methodist Church is not a pacifist church.[16]

While Madsen and Yrigoyen see no claim for pacifism within Article XVI, Long argues precisely the opposite, as noted above. Long claims that the United Methodist Church is constitutionally a pacifist church and posits Article XVI as the basis of that claim.[17] According to Long, the United Methodist Church must reclaim its doctrinal heritage and, in so doing, will return to a pacifist commitment. For Stanley Hauerwas, too, Article XVI positions the United Methodist Church as "a church that seems to be against war."[18] However, he notes later statements contained in the *Book of Discipline* that assert the church's support of people who choose to serve in the armed forces. Hauerwas sees this as a contradiction and likens it to "people who take the wedding vows with their fingers crossed"; he argues that "the Methodists seem to want to have it both ways."[19] It is to these and

---

13. Ibid.

14. Madsen, *This We Believe*, 88.

15. Yrigoyen, *Belief Matters*, 118.

16. Ibid.

17. Long, *Living the Discipline*, 1.

18. Hauerwas, *Dispatches*, 117.

19. Ibid.

other statements on war, peace, and nonviolence—expressed in the Social Principles—that the textual analysis now turns.

The Social Principles

Prior to the 1968 unification between the Methodist Church and the Evangelical United Brethren Church, both churches had statements of social principles. The Methodist Church's "Social Creed" had been adopted in 1908 and was a forerunner and prototype of "The Social Ideals of the Churches" adopted by the Federal Council of Churches during the same year. The Evangelical United Brethren had a statement entitled "Basic Beliefs Regarding Social Issues and Moral Standards" which it adopted in 1946.[20] In 1972, four years after the 1968 unification between of the Methodist Church and the EUB into the United Methodist Church, the General Conference adopted a new statement of Social Principles, which was revised in 1976 and by each consecutive General Conference.[21] While not part of the "Doctrinal Standards" of the United Methodist Church, the Social Principles

> are a prayerful and thoughtful effort on the part of the General Conference to speak to the human issues in the contemporary world from a sound biblical and theological foundation as historically demonstrated in United Methodist traditions. They are a call to faithfulness and are intended to be instructive and persuasive in the best of the prophetic spirit; however, they are not church law. The Social Principles are a call to all members of The United Methodist Church to a prayerful, studied dialogue of faith and practice.[22]

Since the adoption of the new statement of Social Principles in 1972, the Principles have changed, some slightly and others more drastically. The statements concerning war are no exception. What follows is an attempt to show how the statements concerning war and Methodist participation in war have changed since 1968; where available, some commentary regarding how and why those changes occurred is included.

20. Joint Commissions on Church Union, *Constitution for The United Methodist Church*, 37.

21. *Book of Discipline* (2004), 95.

22. Ibid., 95. A change in this description of the Social Principles occurred between the 2000 and 2004 General Conferences. The 2000 *Discipline* does not include the clarification that the Social Principles "are not church law" as does the 2004 *Discipline*.

At the time of the 1968 General Conference uniting the Evangelical United Brethren Church and the Methodist Church, the Methodist Church Social Principle on "The Christian and Military Service" stated that the church "holds within its fellowship those who sincerely differ as to the Christian duty in regard to military service" and "recognize[s] the right of the individual to answer the call of his government according to the dictates of his Christian conscience." It is understood "that non-violent resistance can be a valid form of Christian witness" and that "in all of these situations members of The Methodist Church have the authority and support of their Church."[23]

The EUB social principle on "War and Peace" begins with a much more emphatic denunciation of war as "contrary to the Christian conception of human welfare" and "the basic principles of universal brotherhood." Thus war is "not compatible with the gospel and spirit of Christ"—a phrase which echoes the EUB's Article XVI. However, according to this principle of the EUB, "God alone is the Lord of the conscience. Therefore, the Church recognizes the right of the individual member to answer the call of his government according to the dictates of his conscience and his sense of duty."[24]

In 1972, the General Conference adopted a new set of Social Principles for the United Methodist Church. Speaking specifically about the issue of war are two principles: one is entitled "Military Service" and is found under the section on "The Political Community"; the other is entitled "War and Peace" and is found under the section on "The World Community." Both will be stated in their full form here; subsequent and significant changes made by General Conferences will be described and explained as succinctly as possible.

The 1972 statement on "Military Service" states the following:

> Though coercion, violence, and war are presently the ultimate sanctions in international relations, we reject them as incompatible with the gospel and spirit of Christ. We therefore urge the establishment of the rule of law in international affairs as a means of elimination of war, violence, and coercion in those affairs. We therefore reject national policies of enforced military service in peacetime as incompatible with the gospel. We acknowledge the agonizing tension created by the demand for military service by

23. *Book of Discipline* (1968), 60.
24. Ibid., 66.

national governments. Thus, we support those individuals who
conscientiously oppose all war, or any particular war, and who
therefore refuse to serve in the armed forces. We also support
those persons who conscientiously choose to serve in the armed
forces or to accept alternative service. Pastors are called upon to
be available for counseling with all youth who face conscription
including those who conscientiously refuse to cooperate with a
selective service system.[25]

The statement on "War and Peace" states that:

We believe war is incompatible with the teachings and example
of Christ. We therefore reject war as an instrument of national
foreign policy and insist that the first moral duty of all nations is
to resolve by peaceful means every dispute that arises between or
among them; that human values must outweigh military claims
as governments determine their priorities; that the militarization
of society must be challenged and stopped; and that the manu-

25. *Book of Discipline* (1972), 95. Conversation at the 1972 General Conference
surrounding the adoption of this paragraph reveals the various concerns held among
the delegates. One delegate, Richard Johnson, pushed for an amendment that explicitly
offered the church's full support to those who refused to cooperate with the selective
service system, arguing that he expected the church to "offer me more than the pastoral
counseling that the Committee calls for" (*Journal of the 1972 General Conference of the
United Methodist Church*, 479). Another delegate, Lawton Shroyer, pushed to substitute
his own version of the paragraph on "Military Service." Shroyer's somewhat more pro-
military version reads thus: "We look forward to the day that all people of this world can
live together with Christian love and concern towards each other without the necessity
of an enforced military service. We recognize that military service is part of our responsibility to our beloved nation. We wholeheartedly support those who serve in the armed
forces. In Christian belief, we recognize those individuals who conscientiously oppose all
war and refuse to serve in the armed forces. These conscientious objectors should have
the right to fulfill their duty to their government in alternate and peaceful ways of service
which have been approved by their government" (ibid., 479–80). William Grove offered a
substitute for the last two sentences of the paragraph on "Military Service" which would
succinctly offer equal support to all: "We offer the ministry of the church to those persons
who conscientiously choose to serve in the Armed Forces or to accept alternative service
or who conscientiously refuse to cooperate with the selective service system" (ibid., 480).
At one point in the discussion, according to the General Conference Journal, a gentleman
named Joseph Fichter "observed that the persons who had been debating this issue were
persons who would not be directly affected by it; he stated that the young persons who
would be directly affected should have the dominant voice in the discussion" (ibid.). In
the end, all of the amendments and substitutions under discussion were voted on and
defeated, and the original paragraph proposed by the Committee was adopted.

facture, sale, and deployment of armaments must be reduced and controlled.[26]

In his book *Speak Up for Just War or Pacifism: A Critique of the United Methodist Bishops' Pastoral Letter "In Defense of Creation"*, United Methodist theologian and just war advocate Paul Ramsey recounts the development of the "War and Peace" paragraph in the Social Principles, first adopted by the 1972 General Conference, in order to give "some account of how the United Methodist Church came to adopt into its statement of Social Principles, without much thought about what this would mean in practice, a pacifism that floats above questions of the responsible use of power."[27] Ramsey himself was part of the Study Commission's working group that attended to the "War and Peace" statement of the Social Principles. Referring to the paragraph, Ramsey reports his proposed amendments (none of which were accepted) to the original paragraph which would have avoided the "sweeping pacifist statements"[28] that the paragraph does, in his view, make for the United Methodist Church. According to Ramsey, upon majority acceptance of the paragraph as written by the Commission, a fellow commissioner and social ethics professor noted that if the statement was "adopted by the General Conference, the paragraph would commit our church to a pacifist position for all its sons and daughters, and to a pacifist position for the nation—unilaterally."[29] As a result, argues Ramsey, if the statement on "War and Peace" were taken seriously, it would "mean that Methodist men and women should come out of the armed services and related industries."[30]

Yet in the statement on "Military Service," Ramsey notes that the church extends its support to "those persons who choose to serve in the armed forces."[31] This inconsistency causes Ramsey to state: "Some time ago it ceased to be a Methodist virtue to mean what we say politically by limiting ourselves to saying only what can be meant, and by spelling out how we mean whatever we say to mean."[32] Despite his own acceptance of

26. *Book of Discipline* (1972), 96.
27. Ramsey, *Speak Up*, 7.
28. Ibid., 9.
29. Ibid.
30. Ibid., 8.
31. Ibid., 12.
32. Ibid., 7.

the viability of the just war tradition, Ramsey argues that the doctrinal teaching of the United Methodist Church was, almost from its inception, deeply inconsistent, leading to confusion within the denomination.

In 1976 these two statements were left virtually untouched except for an additional phrase to the "Military Service" statement that gives the church's support not only to those who refuse military service but also to those who refuse "to cooperate with systems of military conscription,"[33] thus making a clear statement about the church's support of conscientious objectors. In 1980 the statements were unchanged except for a clause added to the end of the "War and Peace" statement which specifically addresses the increasing threat posed by nuclear weapons: "and that the production, possession, or use of nuclear weapons be condemned."[34]

In 1984 the statement on "Military Service" was expanded some-what in two different areas. Added to the call for pastors to be available for counseling about conscription is the sentence: "We urge all youth to seek the counsel of the Church as they reach a conscientious decision concerning the nature of their responsibility as citizens." In addition, the statement was expanded from offering "support to those persons who conscientiously oppose all war" to also "extend[ing] the ministry of the Church" to those same persons.[35]

In 1988 the two statements were again left mainly unchanged, as is true of 1992. The 1996 statement on "Military Service" was not changed although the growing indignation of the United Methodist Church against nuclear armament is reflected in an addition to the statement on "War and Peace," which states: "Consequently, we endorse general and complete disarmament under strict and effective international control."[36]

In the 2000 *Book of Discipline* both statements concerning the United Methodist Church response to war are changed rather drastically. These changes were recommended officially to General Conference by Philip Wogaman.[37] Removed from the statement on "Military Service" is the strong language against war that "Though coercion, violence, and war are presently the ultimate sanctions in international relations, we reject

33. *Book of Discipline* (1976), 100.
34. *Book of Discipline* (1980), 103.
35. *Book of Discipline* (1984), 101.
36. *Book of Discipline* (1996), 105.
37. *Journal of the 2000 General Conference of the United Methodist Church*, 1:513–14.

them as incompatible with the gospel and spirit of Christ." In its place, the paragraph-long addition to the statement says:

> We deplore war and urge the peaceful settlement of all disputes among nations. From the beginning, the Christian conscience has struggled with the harsh realities of violence and war, for these evils clearly frustrate God's loving purposes for humankind. We yearn for the day when there will be no more war and people will live together in peace and justice. Some of us believe that war, and other acts of violence, are never acceptable to Christians. We also acknowledge that most Christians regretfully realize that, when peaceful alternatives have failed, the force of arms may be preferable to unchecked aggression, tyranny and genocide. We honor the witness of pacifists who will not allow us to become complacent about war and violence. We also respect those who support the use of force but only in extreme situations and only when the need is clear beyond reasonable doubt, and through appropriate international organizations. We urge the establishment of the rule of law in international affairs as a means of elimination of war, violence, and coercion in these affairs.[38]

The 2000 statement on "War and Peace" was altered as well—but only by the inclusion of one word into the statement. In 2000 this principle states that: "We therefore reject war as a *usual* instrument of national foreign policy. . . ."[39] In his book *To Serve the Present Age: The Gift and Promise of United Methodism*, Wogaman briefly describes the reasoning behind the changes to the two statements. According to Wogaman, just before the 1992 General Conference, he and a small group of theologians met in order to clarify what they understood as "a confused pattern of thought in the church's Social Principles on issues of war and peace."[40] Wogaman notes that the Social Principles describe war as "incompatible" with the gospel and thus "reject war as an instrument of national foreign policy"[41] and admits that these statements appear on the surface to make a pacifist claim for the United Methodist Church. However, Wogaman refers to another statement in the Social Principles entitled "Justice and Law" which states that "Persons and groups must feel secure in their life. . . . Nations, too, must feel secure in the world if world community

38. *Book of Discipline* (2000), 119.
39. Ibid.,121.
40. Wogaman, *To Serve the Present Age*, 78.
41. Ibid.

is to become a fact"[42] in order to explain why war is sometimes justified. Wogaman also cites the support offered to both conscientious objectors and those who choose to serve in the military as negating the claim that the United Methodist Church is a pacifist church. He argues that:

> Most United Methodists, including those who are pacifists, would not classify The United Methodist Church as one of the pacifist denominations. But the pattern of statements in the Social Principles leaves a confused picture. The theologians offered a clarifying amendment acknowledging frankly that some United Methodists stand in the pacifist tradition while others are more persuaded by the "just war" tradition in which military action can be accepted as a last resort if certain moral standards have been met. Such a statement could help clarify the reasons why different members, in good faith, take different positions.[43]

While this discussion took place as early as the 1992 General Conference, it was at the 2000 General Conference that Wogaman was able to move his proposals through General Conference, resulting in a clearer identification of the United Methodist Church with the just war tradition.

Wogaman's statement that he sought to offer "a clarifying amendment acknowledging frankly that some United Methodists stand in the pacifist tradition while others are more persuaded by the 'just war' tradition"[44] seems to suggest that he believes that explaining the fact of the existence of more than one position on war in the *Book of Discipline* helps to clarify any confusion resulting from the multiple views held within the *Discipline*. In other words, Wogaman seems to be saying that an *acknowledgement* of the multiplicity of views serves to explain and elucidate whatever confusion might arise from such pluralism.

The most recent meeting of the General Conference occurred in 2004; at the time of the writing of this study, the 2004 *Discipline* contains the most current authoritative statements for the United Methodist Church. Brief but pertinent changes were made to both statements in the 2004 version. In the statement on "Military Service," the use of the word "most" was replaced by "many" to read thus: "We also acknowledge that many [instead of most] Christians realize that, when peaceful alternatives have failed, the force of arms may regretfully be preferable to unchecked

42. *Book of Discipline* (2000), 121; cited in Wogaman, *To Serve The Present Age*, 78.

43. Wogaman, *To Serve the Present Age*, 79.

44. Ibid.

aggression, tyranny and genocide."[45] At the end of the statement, any leaning in one way or another is checked by the addition of the sentence, "As Christians we are aware that neither the way of military action, nor the way of inaction is always righteous before God."[46]

In the statement on "War and Peace," the word "usual" has quietly disappeared from its position of modifying the use of war as an "instrument of national foreign policy" as it did in the 2000 version. Instead, the statement emphasizes the use of war only as a last resort and reads thus: "We therefore reject war as an instrument of national foreign policy, to be employed only as a last resort in the prevention of such evils as genocide, brutal suppression of human rights, and unprovoked international aggression."[47] This reference to "last resort" further establishes the United Methodist Church as a just war denomination.

GENERAL CONFERENCE RESOLUTIONS ON WAR, PEACE, AND NONVIOLENCE

According to the most recent version of the *Book of Resolutions*, the book "is not legally binding" but "is an official guide from our denomination to be used responsibly for reference, encouragement, study, and support."[48] The *Resolutions* are considered to be "amplifications" of the Social Principles[49] and policy statements of the United Methodist Church. In contrast the *Book of Discipline*, as the "book of law" of the church, carries more weight in terms of authority for United Methodist Christians.

This may very well be the reason that previously-cited scholars who point to inconsistency within United Methodist doctrine and teaching base their judgments on passages from different parts of the *Book of Discipline* and not on the *Book of Resolutions*. However as "amplifications" of the Social Principles (which have been dealt with earlier in this chapter) and as a tool that is intended to guide the church on pertinent issues, a cursory glance at least into the *Book of Resolutions* is fitting. An

45. *Book of Discipline* (2004), 122.

46. Ibid. What is of particular interest here is that the options given in this statement are between either military (and presumably violent) action or no action at all. No option for direct nonviolent action is offered to the Christian.

47. Ibid., 123.

48. *Book of Resolutions* (2004), 24.

49. *Book of Resolutions* (1968), 5.

exhaustive display of resolutions addressing war, peace, and nonviolence would constitute its own chapter and would perhaps suffer from redundancy; instead, a more concise survey of selected materials from the *Book of Resolutions* serves to amplify the multiplicity of positions that already has been shown to exist in the *Book of Discipline*.

In a 1968 resolution entitled "The United Methodist Church and Peace," the church claims that it "has, in the witness of Christ, the key to achieving needed change without violence."[50] Further on, the resolution admits that each person "must decide prayerfully before God what is to be his course of action."[51] Despite initial recognition of the real and available option of nonviolent change—which is acknowledged as being rooted in the person and ministry of Jesus Christ—the church concedes to "hold[ing] within its fellowship persons who sincerely differ at this point of critical decision" and claims that it must "call all to repentance, mediate to all God's mercy, minister to all in Christ's name."[52] Furthermore, the resolution on "The Rule of Law and the Right of Dissent" states: "We affirm the right of nonviolent civil disobedience in extreme cases as a viable option in a democracy and as a sometime requirement for Christians who are to have no other God than the God of Jesus Christ."[53] Here Christ is again lifted up as the norm for Christian ethical decision-making and as the very basis for one's refusal to participate in war; yet a statement elsewhere asserts that "[t]housands of our sons and daughters have, with sincere Christian conscience, responded to the call for service in the military forces."[54] One is left to wonder how the Christ whose witness compels a person to disavow war can be the same Christ around whom another's conscience is formed in such a way that he can feel called readily to participate in war.

---

50. *Book of Resolutions* (1968), 17. Within the "Study Documents" section of the *Book of Resolutions* is a statement entitled "Commendation and Support of the Philosophy of Nonviolence as Established by the Late Dr. Martin Luther King, Jr." Here the United Methodist Church "declares its support of [MLK, Jr.'s] philosophy of nonviolence central to the crusade for freedom which he launched in our midst." Ibid., 87.

51. Ibid., 21.

52. Ibid.

53. Ibid., 42.

54. Ibid., 22.

The first statement of the 1972 *Book of Resolutions* is the "Bishops' Call for Peace and the Self-Development of Peoples."[55] In sixth position among the "Enemies of Peace" is the following paragraph:

> Continued reliance upon military service is an enemy of peace. There have been more war casualties in the twentieth century than in all previous centuries of recorded history combined. Nuclear and biochemical weaponry and new technological war-making equipment have thrust the human race into an indefensible posture. It is alleged that 90 percent of the war casualties in Indochina have been civilian. Old "just war" theories need to be carefully rethought in the light of present reality. Wars fought in the national interest will doubtless continue, but violence begets violence, and in today's world extinction could result from irrational accident or momentary madness.[56]

Later in this same resolution is the admission that "[t]he tradition of nonviolent love is a fundamental dimension of the Christian faith. Christians are challenged to consider and embrace this personal stance, thus providing a redemptive witness in society."[57] A clearer emphasis on and call to nonviolence would be difficult to make.

Concerning statements directly related to war and peace, little new is contained in the 1976 *Book of Resolutions*. Of interest however is that the United Methodist Church for the first time explicitly "declares its opposition to the retention and use of capital punishment and urges its abolition. The use of the death penalty gives official sanction to a climate of violence."[58] In 1980 this topic receives further attention in a resolution that highlights the story from the Gospel of John in which Jesus questions "the moral authority of those who were ready to conduct the execution" of a woman convicted of a crime.[59] The rejection by the United Methodist Church of this type of violence is amplified by the claim that "taking human life . . . violates our deepest belief in God as the creator and the redeemer of humankind. In this respect, there can be no assertion that human life can be taken humanely by the state."[60]

---

55. *Book of Resolutions* (1972), 9.

56. Ibid., 12.

57. Ibid., 15.

58. *Book of Resolutions* (1976), 142.

59. *Book of Resolutions* (1980), 36.

60. Ibid.

In the 1980 resolution on "Certification of Conscientious Objection" the church again explicitly welcomes those who represent different positions on war and violence in its assertion that "[i]t is the responsibility of the Church at all levels to inform its members of the fact that conscientious objection, as well as conscientious participation, is a valid option for Christians."[61] However, an underlying assumption of the value and effectiveness of nonviolence over and against violence seems to be at work in the resolution "Concerning the Draft in the United States" where, in a message to the President of the United States encouraging him to reverse the policy of registration of young people, the United Methodist Church states: "We do not believe that one life, man's or woman's, should be sacrificed in a war in this period of history when the global community provides untapped means for negotiation and the reconciliation of differences."[62]

Despite the somewhat stronger opposition to war expressed in this statement, conversation around a resolution on "The United Methodist Church and Conscription" reveals a check preventing the church from sounding too radical in its statements concerning war. According to the 1980 General Conference Journal, conscription and registration were opposed in both peacetime and wartime in the majority report of the resolution. During debate over the resolution, a minority report was introduced, the presenter of which reasoned that it would be "almost foolhardy" to "take the position that is that extreme."[63] The minority report did "not oppose conscription in war time or registration at any time."[64] In pushing for adoption of the minority report over the majority report, the presenter argued thus: "I would urge you to support the minority report in order that, first, this church does not go on record foolishly to oppose conscription in time of war or national emergency, which may be necessary for the survival of a nation; and two, that we do not take such a position and thereby blunt the validity of our position which is to be against peacetime conscription."[65] In the end, the minority report was adopted by General Conference.

61. Ibid., 38.

62. Ibid., 72.

63. *Journal of the 1980 General Conference of the United Methodist Church*, 1:416.

64. Ibid.

65. Ibid., 417.

Adopted in 1984, the resolution on "Global Racism" makes explicit reference to the use of nonviolent means and methods for dealing with violence: "We affirm the use of non-violent action and resistance as alternatives to human abuse, injustice, war, and exploitation, and that nonviolence become one of the strategies for a new international coalition to combat racism."[66]

In 1988, the resolution "Peace with Justice as a Special Program" is introduced. The resolution highlights the biblical foundations of peace and justice, invoking such prophetic images as "swords into plowshares, peaceable kingdoms, [and] new covenants written on the heart."[67] It also calls forth images of Christ as the "Prince of Peace" and the Kingdom of God as the reign of peace and justice: "It is Christ who ordains a ministry of reconciliation. Repentance prepares us for reconciliation. Then we shall open ourselves to the transforming power of God's grace in Christ. Then we shall know what it means to be 'in Christ.' Then we are to become ambassadors of a new creation, a new Kingdom, a new order of love and justice. (2 Corinthians 5:17–20)"[68] While no explicit reference to nonviolence is made here, the language of "new order" invokes a sense of the unique witness of the Christian community in terms of its response to conflict and violence.

In 1992, the call to nonviolence is made more explicitly once again in the resolution entitled "Justice, Peace, and the Integrity of Creation." In this resolution, the United Methodist Church affirms its support for and participation in the ten World Council of Churches affirmations, one of which states: "We affirm the full meaning of God's peace. We are called to seek every possible means of establishing justice, achieving peace, and solving conflicts by active nonviolence."[69]

The 2000 *Book of Resolutions* introduces a resolution on "Consequences of Conflict." Here one sees a clear turn toward the use of just war teaching as a tool for limiting war: "The United Methodist Church calls upon all who choose to take up arms or who order others to do so to evaluate their actions in accordance with historic church teaching limiting resort to war, including questions of proportionality, legal authority,

66. *Book of Resolutions* (1984), 356.

67. *Book of Resolutions* (1988), 558.

68. Ibid., 559.

69. *Book of Resolutions* (1992), 591–92.

discrimination between combatants and noncombatants, just cause, and probability of success."[70]

In addition, a resolution to "Support Men and Women in the Military" is included in the 2000 version, which states that "General Conference honors, supports, and upholds in our prayers those men and women who serve in our armed services and, in addition, honor and support those United Methodist clergy who serve as chaplains."[71] The process by which this resolution was adopted is particularly interesting in that, according to the 2000 *General Conference Journal*, no conversation was held regarding what it might actually mean to "honor, support, and uphold" people who serve in the armed services. A resolution was submitted by one Kurt Glassco of Oklahoma to the Committee on Agenda and Calendar on May 9th, 2000 during General Conference proceedings. According to the *Journal*, Mr. Glassco offered this resolution "so that there's no misunderstanding in the media."[72] As a long day of talking, listening, and decision-making came to a close on May 12, presiding Bishop Melvin Talbert was attempting not long before the midnight hour to adjourn (in fact had attempted three times to do so) when the chair of the Committee on Agenda and Calendar, Mary Alice Massey, stepped to the microphone to call for a vote on Glassco's proposed resolution (as well as a resolution calling for future General Conferences to budget for professional sign language interpreters). The sense of impatience to end the meeting—and the consequent haste with which the resolution was adopted—can be deciphered in the recorded conversation:

> MASSEY (Florida): There are two resolutions on p. 2283 in the *DCA*, that in good faith we must look at and vote up or down. I promised these people.
>
> BISHOP TALBERT: Identify the page again.
>
> MASSEY: Page 2283, one of them is regarding the men and women in our armed services and the other one is the sign language interpreters and they were not printed earlier, and they're in, and I promised these people that I would bring them to the house's attention before we adjourned.

---

70. *Book of Resolutions* (2000), 762.

71. Ibid., 634.

72. *Journal of the 2000 General Conference of the United Methodist Church*, 4:2244.

BISHOP TALBERT: All right [sic], do you have the page number? Is someone prepared for a motion on these?

MASSEY: I move approval on both resolutions, Bishop.

BISHOP TALBERT: It's seconded. It's before us. Vote when the light appears. You have approved them. [Yes, 683; No, 85] All right, anything further from calendar? All right, secretary.[73]

Especially interesting is the fact that this resolution was voted on and passed simultaneously with a resolution to provide sign language interpreters at General Conference in the future—one to which few would likely have given a negative vote.

A resolution on "Prayer for Military Personnel and for Peace in Iraq," added in 2004, augments the call for support of people in the military by its express resolve to pray "for all military personnel and their families, international leaders and the Iraqi people."[74] Also in 2004, the United Methodist Church refers back to its two Social Principles analyzed earlier in this chapter ("Military Service" and "War and Peace") in its "Rejection of Unilateral First-Strike Actions and Strategies." Using the Social Principles as the basis for such rejection, the church launches a condemnation of the war in Iraq; "by attacking Iraq without the approval and participation of the United Nations, the United States has squandered its positive reputation as a responsible member of the global community in the effort to make the world safe for democracy, instigating instead, a wide-spread mood of resentment and an attitude of mistrust toward Americans."[75]

CONCLUSION: INCLUSION OR CONFUSION?

The purpose of this chapter has been to demonstrate through textual analysis of United Methodist doctrine that the doctrine is pluralistic and even self-contradicting in its teachings on war and peace. While some statements exist which indicate a nonviolent or pacifist stance, many other statements indicate a just war stance. Nonviolence is sometimes noted as a position that is honored and supported by the denomination, but it is not understood as a necessary requirement of Christian faith, discipleship, or membership in the United Methodist Church.

73. Ibid., 2472–73.
74. *Book of Resolutions* (2004), 841.
75. Ibid., 850.

Given the pluralism of views on war and peace contained within the doctrine, how one might judge this state of affairs is the subject of the following few paragraphs. The views of scholars on both sides of this question were discussed in chapter 3 and highlighted at various points throughout the current chapter; only a brief review of the argument is provided here as a point of departure for dealing with the questions raised by the fact of doctrinal plurality. These questions are in turn addressed in chapter 6.

For some scholars, doctrinal plurality in the United Methodist Church is considered fitting and appropriate for a denomination that is inclusive, open, and always forming and changing in the light of new contexts and ideas (Thomas Langford, Albert Outler). For others, such plurality within church doctrine is a source of confusion and instability and threatens the credibility of the church's moral witness (John Cobb, Jr., Scott Jones).

Particularly regarding issues of war and nonviolence, a few key Methodist scholars speak to the issue, with several standing in disagreement with one another. Thomas Frank maintains that "the Social Principles reflect and reinforce the United Methodist effort to hold the middle ground on social issues. This stance sometimes requires taking virtually opposite positions on the same issue."[76] To illustrate this point, Frank points to three issues addressed within the Social Principles: homosexuality, abortion, and war and peace. Philip Wogaman views the state of current United Methodist doctrine as creating space for those who take up the nonviolent or pacifist standpoint and those who advocate for the just war tradition. Wogaman understands this as a positive situation based on his assertion that "[b]oth views can be expressed with theological depth. In the church's teaching on war and peace . . . it is helpful to keep both traditions before us."[77]

Stanley Hauerwas, on the other hand, vehemently argues that one "simply cannot mix just war and pacifism and have a consistent position."[78] In one of his more organic analogies, Hauerwas argues that "it is no easier to be a little bit pacifist than it is to be a little bit pregnant."[79] He wonders

---

76. Frank, *Polity, Practice, and the Mission of the United Methodist Church*, 153–54.

77. Wogaman, *To Serve the Present Age*, 79.

78. Hauerwas in Ramsey, *Speak Up*, 167.

79. Ibid., 156.

"why Christians so often say they are advocates of peace but accept the necessity of war" and how it is that they can "acknowledge the nonviolent character of the Gospel while continuing to support Christian participation in war."[80] To assume that war is sometimes a necessity means for Hauerwas that "just war, as a theory, denies pacifism; it does not attempt to make war impossible, but rather to make the moral necessity of war serve human purposes."[81]

Despite the fact of doctrinal plurality, statements within the written sources of doctrine themselves seem to call for greater consistency and uniformity when it comes to ethical quandaries and teachings. In arguing for "the connection between doctrine and ethics," the church itself states in its own *Book of Discipline* that "a church lacking the courage to act decisively on personal and social issues loses its claim to moral authority."[82] Likewise, the *Book of Resolutions* claims that the Social Principles "are declarations to help us be in dialogue with one another about how faith motivates us to 'get off the fence' and act."[83] This is rather strong language for the denomination if doctrinal plurality is good and right, as some scholars claim.

A brief look at the relationship between doctrine and ethics as they pertain to the church's response to another major issue provokes thought and discussion as well. As D. Stephen Long points out, "language similar to that of Article XVI is used by the United Methodist Church to prohibit homosexual activity."[84] Long is referring to the Social Principles statement on "Human Sexuality," which states succinctly that "The United Methodist Church does not condone the practice of homosexuality and consider [sic] this practice *incompatible* [italics mine] with Christian teaching."[85] As such, "self-avowed practicing homosexuals are not to be certified as candidates, ordained as ministers, or appointed to serve in The United Methodist Church."[86] Furthermore, "practices declared by The United Methodist Church to be *incompatible* [italics mine] with Christian teach-

80. Hauerwas, *Against the Nations*, 186.

81. Ibid., 192.

82. *Book of Discipline* (2004), 49.

83. *Book of Resolutions* (2004), 24.

84. Long, *Living the Discipline*, 1n1.

85. *Book of Discipline* (2004), 101.

86. Ibid., 197.

ings" include "being a self-avowed practicing homosexual," "conducting ceremonies which celebrate homosexual unions" and "performing same-sex wedding ceremonies"; they are so incompatible, in fact, that a bishop or clergy-person can be brought to trial for any of these offenses.[87] In the words of Long, this "only provides further warrant that any consistent reading of Article XVI commits the United Methodist Church to pacifism."[88]

The Social Principles state that "war is incompatible with the teachings and example of Christ." Article XVI of the Confession of Faith states that "war and bloodshed are contrary to the gospel and spirit of Christ." This is strong language if the denomination is simply trying to remain "open" in its doctrinal teachings. To state that something is "incompatible" with another is to assert that those two positions are "unable to be true simultaneously" and "unable to be held simultaneously by one person."[89] Furthermore, to state that one thing is "contrary" to another means that it is "opposite in nature or character."[90] What can be said about a church that so precisely labels the institution of war as a *complete opposite* to that which is Christ-like, but then blesses and supports the decision of governments and individuals to engage in some wars and violence? What does it mean that church doctrine names war as *contrary* to Christ but then condones war by sending off its own to be players in carrying out war's violence and destruction? What does it mean that the doctrine of the church can be used to remove a homosexual clergy-person from his or her post but then holds no sway over clergy who are publicly supportive of a particular war or any war? Any consistent reading of the language of "incompatibility" and "contrary" within the doctrine would seem to indicate that church members are actively and knowingly complicit in sin when they fight in a war. To argue otherwise means that war is not always and actually incompatible with the gospel of Christ—and neither would be the ordination and ministry of practicing homosexual clergy.

Yet important questions remain about what a firm standing in one or the other direction on the moral issue of war and nonviolence would mean for the church. If the 2008 General Conference decided that the *Discipline*

---

87. Ibid., 719.

88. Long, *Living the Discipline*, 1n1.

89. *Random House College Dictionary*, 673.

90. Ibid., 292.

should be re-written to exclude all reference to the validity of just war thinking, should those who support the just war be shunned or excommunicated? How would or should the church minister to those who disagree with its doctrine? Where is the line between acceptance of diversity, on one hand, and theological and doctrinal purity, on the other?

The question then remains: at best, either the doctrine of the United Methodist Church on issues of war and nonviolence is demonstrative of an appropriately inclusive and open ecclesiology in which differing views can and should be held together, or at worst, is indicative of widespread confusion about how Methodists are to respond to the moral issues of war and violence. This question in part drives the qualitative aspect of this study, which aims to draw out the lived theology of nonviolence among Methodists who hold a commitment to nonviolence and to bring it into dialogue with the questions raised by the textual analysis of United Methodist doctrine.[91] Understanding this lived theology is the subject of the following chapter.

91. It is important to reiterate that this is not the only point of the qualitative interviews and analysis. The lived theology approach will also serve to spell out some of the theological foundations and practices for nonviolence which, if the doctrine is rightly open and inclusive, should be included in dialogue within the church about how Methodists might think and act when it comes to the moral issues of war and nonviolence.

5

Qualitative Analysis: Findings and Report

INTRODUCTION

THIS CHAPTER PROVIDES A report of findings from the qualitative analysis. In order to organize, focus, and clearly present these findings, the report is organized based on answers to interview questions asked of participants during data collection. Each interview question is re-stated below and is followed by a composite answer based on the answers supplied by interviewee-participants. Such organization is a recognized and valid option for reporting qualitative data, "especially where a standardized interviewing format was used."[1] Following the report of answers to individual interview questions, the original central research questions are re-stated and answered. In line with phenomenological methodology, the findings are presented here in a narrative "creative synthesis" which is "the bringing together of the pieces that have emerged [from the data] into a total experience [of a particular phenomenon], showing patterns and relationships."[2] In accordance with the terms of the Informed Consent Form (Appendix A), which promise anonymity of interviewees, study participants are designated only by the letter "P" for "Participant" and an assigned number (for example, Participant 2 is noted as P2) throughout this chapter.

---

1. Patton, *Qualitative Research*, 439.

2. Ibid., 487. It is important to note that, given such a small sample, valid generalizations based on gender, race, age, or other demographic differences cannot be made. The study is meant to initiate a dialogue between United Methodist practitioners of nonviolence and the doctrine of the church; therefore answers to the central questions are provided in broad strokes.

How do United Methodists define and understand their commitments to nonviolence?

With regard to how practitioners define Christian nonviolence and describe their commitments, three main characteristics or themes arise from the interviews. First, practitioners see nonviolence as *central to Christian faith*; it is an integral part of what it means to identify authentically as a disciple of Christ. Second, nonviolence is *dynamic*; it is understood to be active in the face of injustice or violence, to be creative in its development of nonviolent strategies, and to be effective in the implementation of those strategies. This notion of nonviolence undercuts the assumption of passivity that is sometimes associated with nonviolence and pacifism. Third, nonviolence is defined as *comprehensive*; it is a way of being or living in the world that seeks connectedness and relationality with other people, with the created order, and with God. Consistent with scholarship cited in chapter 3, nonviolence is not simply a response to the moral problem of war but is understood to be a broader way of life.

Central to Christian Faith

As one participant described it, coming to the commitment to nonviolence is a sign of a maturing Christian faith (P7). While one woman conceded her belief that it was possible for people to be nonviolent apart from a "particular religious tradition," she explained that for herself, the commitment to nonviolence certainly arose out of her "faith perspective" (P6). Three other participants went so far as to describe nonviolence and Christian faith as inseparable. One stated that "I'm a pacifist because I'm a Christian. And I don't think that I would be if I wasn't a Christian. And I find it difficult to understand those who are Christians who aren't nonviolent people. So, I consider nonviolence to be really at the heart of my faith" (P4). Similarly, another asserted that he does not believe in "nonviolence" apart from the qualifier *Christian*: "I don't think that that's possible. Now, Christian nonviolence, I would define that as somebody who is taking Jesus seriously enough to see his nonviolence, and attempt to follow it. So, very Christocentric, if you want. I honestly don't think that apart from Christ, one can be—or can even understand—the concept of nonviolence" (P10). The third participant—and also the youngest of the twelve people interviewed—described his "experience of feeling like nonviolence is—I mean an incredibly central part of . . . how we're called to love one another as Christians" (P8).

Dynamic

The characteristic of "dynamic" is intended to encapsulate descriptions such as "active," "effective," "practical," and "creative." Participants described a wish to "mend the world" (P6), to express "concern for the other" (P2), to respond to "situations of injustice . . . and sometimes very actively so" (P5), and "to be open to talking, to dialoguing, to new understanding, to working out solutions together" (P3). Participants also expressed the view that nonviolence is the most "effective way of dealing with conflict situations" (P5) and "work[ing] for change" (P3); put simply, nonviolence really does "work" (P4, P10). In their assertions that there is always another way of dealing with difficult situations (P6, P11) and that there is an "art" to doing so (P4), participants also noted the need for creativity and imagination in nonviolent action. The following interview excerpt provides a helpful and comprehensive understanding of the dynamic nature of the nonviolent commitment:

> I think that when I talk about pacifism or nonviolence, it doesn't mean, as I said, non-confrontational. I think that I look at the examples from South Africa, and [Martin Luther] King in America, nonviolent, you know, demonstrations, and sending emails or letters. There are ways to confront injustice, and to confront evil, and to speak truthfully without that resorting into violence. I've got a list of 200 different acts of resistance, nonviolent resistance. And so when you say pacifism . . . that doesn't mean you're a doormat. It doesn't mean that you just lay down and let people walk all over you and do whatever they want. . . . It means just not reacting violently, but you can still—there are ways to go about bringing about change and, you know, confronting the oppressor without using violence. . . .It invites conflict and it invites you to get into conflict, but just not using violence." (P4)

Comprehensive

Finally, participants define nonviolence in holistic and relational terms. A few participants referred explicitly to violence as more than physical harm alone (P9, P2, P11). Others described nonviolence as a "way of being" or "living" or "acting" in the world (P8, P1, P3, P7). A number of participants further noted the connectedness they see between a nonviolent way of life and other areas of life, which further justifies the view that nonviolence is much more than a response to the specific problem of war. Nonviolence relates to the care of God's creation (P1, P11), to other ethical issues of life and death such as abortion, euthanasia, and the death penalty (P10), to education and healthcare (P11, P12), to economics (P1, P11), and to a sense of overall relationality and connectedness between people (P8, P1, P2, P3, P11, P12). One participant emphasized this sense of connectedness in her wonderfully comprehensive definition of nonviolence:

> Perhaps I would define it as caring for all of creation, caring for self, caring for others, and recognizing the divine in all things. So, I think my understanding of nonviolence really has widened to be inclusive of the way I am in the world, the way I am with myself, and the way I am with other people, the way I try to live a balanced life in terms of rest and work and play, quiet solitude, mindfulness, so that I don't do violence to myself by overworking. So, I've come to see nonviolence in terms of what we do to ourselves, as well as how we are in relationship with one another, whether it's here or somewhere else in the world. So, I think it's widened, and it's in process. . . . It's definitely in process, but I think nonviolence has to do with treating myself and others gently, with respect, with honor, and mindfulness of God who is in all.
>
> And it affects what I purchase, who I purchase it from, how I eat . . . how I choose to spend my money. All of those things I see as related to being in the world in a nonviolent way. So, it's—it's a very big question.
>
> And it continues to grow. As I read and reflect on other people, and how they're living their lives in terms of nonviolence, I'm coming to see more and more how the way I spend my money—if I choose to own a vehicle, for instance—has a tremendous effect on contributing to the violence that's in the world right now. The Middle East, our hunger for oil, the things that we support and . . . we are not always even aware that we're helping to support that whole industry, so that in North America, our hunger for energy and power helps to feed violence in other places, and I'm beginning to see more and more how my life and the choices I make contribute to that, or may help. I'm hoping with new choices, different choices may contribute towards a new reality. That's a hope. It's still a long way away. (P1)

The Limitations of Nonviolence

The level to which interviewees defined themselves as either condition-
ally nonviolent, on one end of the spectrum, or radically nonviolent on
the other end, was not specifically addressed by the interview questions;
however, this issue did arise on its own in three conversations. Two participants admitted that they did not view themselves as absolutely pacifist
or nonviolent. The first, a mother of grown children, questioned how
she might react if one of her children was attacked but believed that she
"would definitely try to use words first and negotiate things" before resorting to violence (P6). The second said that he could "see some situations
where violence may be the least evil thing of the possible options" but
considered himself to be "relatively pacifist in that nonviolence is usually
not only the most moral but also the most effective way of dealing with
conflict situations" (P5).

Only one participant took the more radical stance of absolute non-
defense, although he did admit that his nonviolence had never been tested
in a significant way: "I would even hope that . . . my faith, you know, would
be strong enough that I'd be willing to die. You know, Jesus himself, when-
ever he was being arrested, his disciples start coming out swinging. And
he says, 'Put your sword away.' And he heals the guy who had his ear cut
off. Refuses to defend himself violently. And he's killed for it. And I think
that's part of the commitment when you say that you're a pacifist and
you're trying to live that out is that you may be killed for it. You hope not.
But that was the way of the Master, so why shouldn't it be the way of the
servant as well?" (P4).

INTERVIEW QUESTION TWO:

*What are the Scriptural, theological, and non-Christian sources that
undergird the commitment to nonviolence?*

The lived theologies of nonviolence among United Methodist Christians
have strong Scriptural and theological roots. As the data reveal, theologies of nonviolence are tied particularly to the teachings and example
of Jesus Christ, Biblical conceptions of forgiveness, and Biblical images
of peace. Christian nonviolence, as defined and practiced by this study's
interviewee-participants, is also rooted in the example of the early
Christian church, ecclesiological views, eschatology, and other theological categories. For some participants, sources that lie outside the realm of

the category "Christian" have served to shape in part a theology of and commitment to nonviolence.

Foundations in Scripture

When asked which Scripture passages were central in a theology of nonviolence, most interviewees pointed to texts related to the teachings and example of Jesus Christ. Many referenced the teachings of Jesus, particularly the Sermon on the Mount (Matthew 5:1–7:29) (P5, P8, P1, P6, P4, P7) and his reading of the Isaiah scroll at the start of his public ministry (Luke 4:16-21) (P5, P12). Jesus' nonresistance and nonviolent response to his own arrest and execution stands as a primary example and model for nonviolent United Methodist Christians (Matthew 26:47–56; Mark 14:43–49; Luke 22:47-53) (P2, P5, P6, P4, P10). The clear and perhaps unquestioning reliance on Jesus' teachings and example as central to the nonviolent commitment is captured by one interviewee's statement: "Like even the night that . . . Jesus was arrested and he said, 'those who live the sword will die by the sword.' I mean you take that for what it says. It's not a very complicated thing. It is pretty straightforward. And the beatitudes are pretty straightforward things" (P8).

Biblical conceptions of forgiveness were also central in interviewees' nonviolent commitments. These conceptions include Jesus' teachings on forgiveness, such as the parable of the debtor (Matthew 18:23–35) (P9), his frequent and scandalous associations with prostitutes and tax collectors (P4), and his words of forgiveness to his executioners as he died on the cross (Luke 23:34) (P6). Romans 12 was referenced for its directives about the necessity of forgiveness for life in Christian community (P4). Participants also reached back into the Hebrew Scriptures, where the story of Joseph's reconciliation with his brothers after they sold him into slavery is noted as a central story of forgiveness (Genesis 45) (P1, P2).

Other classic notions of nonviolence and more generally, of peace, abound. Interviewees pointed to the prophet Isaiah's call "to beat swords into ploughshares" (Isaiah 2:4) (P1, P6), and to Micah 6:8, where the prophet asks, "And what does the Lord require of you but to do justice, and to love kindness, and to walk humbly with your God?" (P6, P9, P12). From the Pentateuch, sources of nonviolence include the Ten Commandments (Exodus 20) (P4) and the story of receiving the stranger (Genesis 19) (P9).

The description by one interviewee of a particular Scripture passage seemed not only to express the importance of the passage for her understanding of nonviolence, but also resonates clearly with interviewees' broad definitions of nonviolence, as reported earlier in this chapter. Here she describes in her own words the passage from Genesis 26:17–33:

> I stumbled on the story once . . . it's the story of the well, and of others coming to the well, and they were not of that tribe. They were not of that group, and . . . they were ready for conflict. The resolution was to dig another well—to dig another well. And that story for me . . . [is a] story of problem-solving by really trying to lean into the notion of there needing to be enough resources for all people. So, instead of fighting, finding more resources, and sharing the resources that were there. I love that story, and that whole notion of enough, that as we are connected with everyone, we really cannot be satisfied until others have enough. If we have enough, then we have to make sure others have enough, too. (P1)

One can clearly see the notions of action and creativity, concern for and connectedness to others, and the practical and effective nature of nonviolence at work in her reading of this particular Scripture passage.

Theological Underpinnings

A strong theology of creation is at the heart of the commitment to nonviolence for several study participants, although participants' views exhibit particular nuances. For one individual, war and conflict are an abhorrence because they destroy God's creation: "I don't believe that our Creator created this wonderful creation for us to destroy it. So that's where specific wars or conflicts . . . don't fit into that picture, because of the devastation that it does, because of the fact that it is not honoring and respecting the people" (P1). For another, a theology of creation humbles humanity's will to power by providing a sense that there is something "bigger than whatever the situation is, that we belong to God in our flaws and whatever it is that we're doing, and so that whatever the situation is, there's something beyond that that's important" (P11). Creation by God also implies a common human nature, which has implications for how people relate to fellow human beings: "But the vision is fullness and love and connectedness and understanding that I am a part of you. I don't want that part of me that is in you to hurt. I realize that whatever I do resonates with you and it, in turn, comes back" (P12). This notion of a common human nature and its implications are carried further by another participant:

> I think that if a person has committed murder, or done something horrible . . . theologically, I understand that I am exactly like that person in that I am capable of doing the same evil, that we're created as these wonderful creatures, but just like that person murdered, I'm capable of murder. You know? I pray to God I never do it, but it's not like they're a separate species from me. So, it's an understanding of common humanity; there but for the grace of God go I, and trying to deeply understand them. And so, I do wonder how someone without that theological concept, how do—what leads them to love the enemy, love the other person?" (P3)

A number of interviewees rooted their commitments in an understanding of the practices of the early Christian church. The nonviolent existence of the early church in a militarized and violent surrounding culture is viewed as "counter-cultural" (P10) and "prophetic Christianity" (P7) and "a more faithful way" (P4). Unfortunately, under Constantine "the mainstream of the church became much more concerned about defending civilization and, therefore, step by step, inch by inch, agreeing to join in [the] military and, finally, encouraging the military, and often becoming indistinguishable from secular rationales for armed force in defense of the empire later on in the nation state" (P5).

For some nonviolent United Methodists, a strong theology of resurrection and eschatology is vital to the nonviolent commitment. While one interviewee pointed more generally to an understanding of a "broader framework of the kingdom of God" (P5), others expressed a further developed view that a belief in resurrection allows freedom from the fear of death. One participant explained that to be truly nonviolent, Christians "have to be at some point in our faith where we're not afraid of death, and we do not see it as an end." Belief in resurrection creates the possibility for a person to refuse to engage in violence in order to defend life; "it makes it possible to understand life properly, that life has no need for violence" (P10). Another interviewee stated his theology of resurrection in this way:

> I have a lot of trouble articulating why I believe in nonviolence to someone . . . without being in a Christian framework because for me the argument . . . kind of begins and ends with, you know, you might die and that really wouldn't be the worst thing that could

happen, which is not something that plays well for most people unless . . . you're standing on a promise of resurrection. . . . So . . . nonviolence is definitely a big commitment of faith to me because it talks about, you know, rather than doing everything I can think of to preserve my well-being and my life, I will trust in what God has said about what are the means for how we ought to live and trust that whatever end may come, there's a greater end and a greater purpose to that. And . . . one reason that I think nobody has any understanding of nonviolence is that we don't talk about martyrs at all and . . . we say at every Easter that death is not the final word but then we tend to act like it is. (P8)

Again, the teachings and example of Jesus Christ play a key role in how nonviolent United Methodists understand their commitments.[3] In the words of one participant, "I want Christians to take Jesus seriously" (P10). To do so means "following in Christ's footsteps, and what his call is for us" (P4). And when faced with violence and persecution, "he reacted with nonviolence" (P10). Carrying the example of Christ as normative for contemporary Christians a bit further, one woman said:

I think that very clearly, that what we understand of Jesus is that that's how he was in the world, that [is how] he was in terms of standing with the people that were oppressed, people on the margins, whether that was . . . women, or poor folks, or tax collectors, or whoever, there was a sense of his making a real strong stand against those that would do harm, while at the same time, evidently having a remarkable ability to continue to love one's enemy, and I think that would be how I would understand that now in terms of what it means to love one's enemy. It's not to let your enemy walk all over you, or anybody else—to stop that, but to be open to caring about them as a person. (P3)

Finally, there exists a particular ecclesiological view within the nonviolent commitment—an ecclesiology that is open to disagreement and, through its openness to dialogue and discussion about difficult issues, seeks to draw people closer to the goal of Christian discipleship. Some study participants highlighted the idea of the "Body of Christ" and the

3. The teachings of Jesus were also noted as central to interviewees' understandings of nonviolence in the previous section on "Foundations in Scripture." The findings here are abstracted from isolated references to Scripture and therefore have been placed under the category of "Theological Underpinnings" because they more generally are concerned with interpretations of the biblical Jesus, his teachings, and the meaning of both for thinking about nonviolence.

diversity that must exist within the Body (P8, P6, P11). As one participant suggested, "I guess that I want a church that has a lot of room for a lot of people. . . . I really appreciate the diversity in the United Methodist Church and want it all to be there. I just don't want one voice to drown out other voices" (P6). Two participants referred to the same concrete example to demonstrate their open sense of what it means to be the church. At a conference of the United Methodist Church held near Springfield, Massachusetts some years ago, a group of young people met another young man whose father was an official in the Ku Klux Klan; upon learning of this, the group wrote and submitted a resolution to General Conference that any person affiliated with a hate group could not be a member of the United Methodist Church. For one participant, this was "not acceptable, because number one, where is the best place for them? The church! That's our function, I think, and also if you use this against this particular hate group this year, it might be people who part their hair on the right side the next time around" (P2). According to the other participant, "I remember being part of the conversation with some of those young people when they brought what they wanted to do to Annual Conference, because—I mean, there's so much involved in that, you know? Is that the point of membership? And how do you—is it that you're saying you can't be a United Methodist and be a member of a hate group? I would hope you wouldn't be. I know that people are, but I think that we work together around that. It's not an excuse, but hopefully, [we] find ways to help people grow into a different place" (P11). This is a particularly poignant illustration of the need for an open ecclesiology when one considers that both of these participants are themselves African American.

One participant described how she came into a new kind of openness when she set out to undercut the power and theology of the conservative and far-right voices in the United Methodist Church.

> I was outraged at what they were doing. . . . But in the process of researching what they were doing, an interesting thing happened to me internally in that . . . the more I researched and studied what they were doing, the better I came to understand them, and why they were doing what they were doing. And the deeper grew my commitment to not demonize these folks, and to do to them what I feel they're doing to those of us on the left. So, it was ironically setting out to do a project to expose the wicked deeds [laughter] of these folks on the right, which caused me to go through an internal

process of . . . understanding what the church is about. . . . I didn't want to just turn the tables, and tell falsehoods, and demonize, and not understand these other folks. So . . . that's a very distinct thing, where I can point to, and say I went through a process of starting out with [the notion that] we've got to expose these bastards, to ending up . . . giving a very sympathetic presentation of how they had felt like a minority, why they were doing what they were doing, and yet, saying this is very dangerous for the church. (P3)

Following this theme of an open church, one participant puts it more concisely: "even when we try to shut out people that disagree with us, I feel like we're destroying the Body of Christ and making small what God is trying to open up and give us" (P6). Similarly, one participant explained:

I think that that's, you know, what it means to be kind of the church universal, that we don't agree on things but that we still will struggle to try to come together, that we've been given the gift, the ministry of reconciliation. And so we use that. And even though we don't agree, we can still worship together and can still be in dialogue about these issues, you know, preferably, hopefully, through holy conversation maybe someday we will agree on that. But rather than every disagreement, you know, [causing a] splitting off from the church and doing one's own thing, I think it is good that we have this kind of commitment to our church. . . But, you know, that's kind of a tricky thing, sending someone away from the community. I mean you wouldn't—you'd really never want to do that because I don't think that God ever really gives up on people. So, as a church, do we want to ever really give up on someone? I would say no. (P4)

Non-Christian Foundations

Briefly, the sources of nonviolence that were named by participants which are not *Christian* must be noted; these sources also serve to shape and sustain the commitment to nonviolence for those United Methodists who hold to that commitment. Some participants point to nonviolent teachings that spring from other religious traditions such as Native American spirituality (P1), eastern meditative traditions such as those involved in some forms of Hinduism and Buddhism (P1, P6), and the teachings and practices of Gandhi (P1, P6, P10). Some point to twelve-step programs as important models of "mutual struggle . . . and affirmation" (P6) or to secular models of social justice advocacy (P12) as influential in their commitments to a broader conception of nonviolence. And two participants simply pointed to the practical failures of war and violence as a remedy for contemporary problems, insisting that there must be some better way to address such problems (P8, P3). By way of analogy for doing away with that which does not work, one participant noted the failures of the prison system and asserted: "Our prison system doesn't work, so even if I had no theological basis for this, even if I had not grown up in a family that . . . tried to emulate [Martin Luther] King—even if none of that was there, I would think from a practical standpoint [that] you look at a prison system, where recidivism is so high, and you say, well, I wonder if we did it this way, if it would—if it worked better" (P3).

Interview Question Three:

What are the practices of nonviolence among United Methodists who hold and sustain that commitment?

The question of how practitioners actually *live out* their faith convictions about nonviolence drives a discussion of practices. In naming and describing their practices of nonviolence, interviewees point to a wide variety of activities which range from those carried out in the quiet of one's personal time and space, to those performed within the context of communal worship and other church gatherings, to activities executed in the political and public spheres, where interviewees seek to witness to God's presence and sovereignty in the wider world. Many of these practices cut across all three of these areas (for example, prayer and speaking up against injustice); as a result, the variety of practices of nonviolence described by interviewees lends support to the conclusions drawn in the first section of this chapter that nonviolent United Methodists define and understand the commitment to nonviolence as a comprehensive and holistic way of life. To state this another way, the fact that the practices of nonviolence cut across so many areas of life directly relates to the view of interviewees that nonviolence is defined not solely as a response to the particular problem of war but is understood to be a way of life that connects to relationships with self, others, the creation, and God.

Prayer, Stillness, and Related Practices

Not surprisingly, prayer is a central practice for those United Methodists who identify as nonviolent (P1, P6, P7, P8). In the words of one participant, "I feel like that's like a baseline, base level thing that I ought to be doing as a Christian, is praying for my brothers and sisters around the world who are living in the face of day-to-day violence" (P8). Another described the effect of prayer on the internal change necessary to be a nonviolent person: "if I can't be peaceful in my own heart, then it's not going to come out as peaceful towards others" (P6). Participants also named practices that are often associated with prayer, such as silence and reflection (P1) and meditation (P5, P6). Reading was considered an important practice for two participants (P1, P5); one said that reading the lectionary allowed "God's spirit to reformulate my spirit and bring it into harmony" (P5). Other practices included journaling and radical simplicity (P1) and regular spiritual retreats (P6); Sabbath-keeping created space for one participant to "release the world from being my responsibility . . . [by] just being still and letting God run the world for a day. . . . I think that that's a form of nonviolence for me because it gets me off of my driven-ness, and off of my agendas, and my self-envisioned importance, and overzealous responsibility and things like that. So, it's a day that humility and receptivity reign" (P6).

Another important practice involved "becoming more aware of the ways in which [one is] not nonviolent" and a willingness to be confronted when one fails to be nonviolent (P11). In a similar vein, one participant called for "the acceptance of responsibility and the acknowledgement of personal sin . . . rather than a self-righteous attitude, which is sometimes too common even among people who are pacifists or nonviolent. They feel prideful in their superior morality" (P5). Learning humility is an important practice both in sustaining one's own commitment to nonviolence and in encouraging others along that path.

The Importance of Communities

Three participants described the communities of which they are a part and the role that particular communities of nonviolent Christians have played in shaping her or his understanding of nonviolence (P1, P3, P4). Others explained the ways in which the practice of being connected to a nonviolent community is, in fact, imperative for sustaining the commitment to nonviolence. As one put it straightforwardly, "The only way to be nonviolent is to live within the community who promotes nonviolence, I think" (P10). Another connected the importance of community to his vision of the human condition: "That's life, you know. If we miss the target of participating in God's shalom, we're going to be thrown back on ourselves; and that is to choose solitude, and to choose solitude is to choose death. We're made for a community" (P12).

Practices in the Context of Worship

A number of practices were named by interviewees which occur specifically within the context of the Christian community's corporate worship. The practice of gathering in corporate worship itself was seen as an important practice (P3, P10). Eucharist is a central nonviolent practice within worship because it involves "lifting up the body and blood of Christ which was given as gift in the face of violence; we're celebrating the resurrected life, which was God's answer to our violence. . . . The liturgy itself is a declaration of nonviolence" (P10). Furthermore, eucharist allows people to "look and see black people and white people and . . . poor people and rich people coming to God's table, and coming forward with your hands outstretched, empty, and sharing in literally one loaf" (P4).

The practice of preaching was by far one of the most-discussed practices for nonviolent United Methodists. For one pastor, it was as straightforward as "trying to mold a culture, at least in this congregation and in every other place I have influence, to help people to think again about presumptions and prejudices that they had held to be true and challenge those" (P6). Two participants—one pastor and one layperson—highlighted the accountability for one's own behavior that is built in to the practice of preaching nonviolence. As one suggested, "part of the reason why I talk about [nonviolence] a lot [is] so that people can hold me accountable when the time comes" (P4); similarly, the other asserted that preaching "forces you to conform to your words because other people hear you say them. In other words it's an accountability thing" (P10).

Of particular interest in the emphasis on preaching is the difficulty surrounding the practice of what many interviewees referred to as *prophetic* preaching. Over and over again, participants who are currently or have been pastors noted both the importance of and obstacles to preaching a nonviolent message in their churches (P1, P6, P11, P4, P7, P10, P12). The following experience was relayed by a clergy woman who is not currently serving a local church but was doing so during the First Persian Gulf War:

> I was serving a congregation with all kinds of people, who had all
> kinds of different points of view, and for whom the bombings seen
> on television was kind of like being at a football game or a video
> game or something. And it was very hard. So, I preached what I
> needed to preach. I felt I was trying to be true to myself, but also
> offered conversation times for people with all points of view to
> come and have a conversation, but it isn't easy when people have
> such very, very different points of view, and very passionate points
> of view. And they clearly just think you're really wrong. And you
> have no right to say what you say. So, those of course are difficult
> times in the local church. It isn't easy being the pastor of a local
> church. It just isn't, regardless of what the issue is. But when this
> one really hits, it's very hard to walk gently with the passion and yet
> honor people where they are without damaging them, too. (P1)

Another pastor read from Mark Twain's *The War Prayer* during a
worship service, which angered some parishioners. The lesson for the
pastor was that, "It's the toss-up between a prophetic voice and a pastoral voice. And when I get strong on the prophetic side and forsake the
pastoral dimension, things get out of whack here. And so I'm always having to try to hold those two together" (P6). Another pastor realized "the
honeymoon was over" one Sunday when he preached a sermon entitled
"When the Flag Gets Bigger Than the Cross." While he received a more
favorable response from some than expected, he also "got threats to leave
the church" (P12). One pastor described the temptation to avoid this difficulty: "And you can avoid the hard words that need to be said . . . I try
to do lectionary preaching, and if something's just happened in the world,
where there's war . . . and the Biblical passage is calling me . . . to make a
statement around peace, you know, but it's easy not to do that. . . . I mean,
nobody is telling you [that] you have to preach it a certain way" (P11).

The tension that exists regarding just how far a pastor should be
willing to go in being prophetic is illustrated by the conversations with
two participants in particular. One argued that pastors "are afraid to be
prophetic because they don't want to get people angry at them. . . . You
have to be faithful and not worry about what the people in the pews are
going to think about what you say. But you just have to be faithful to the
gospel. And there are so many pastors and other folks that are afraid to
do that because they're not going to be liked as much and it's going to
cause problems for them to come out and to say that war is wrong. And
so just to begin that discussion more, and have more folks that are willing

to make statements like that, to get people thinking" (P4). However, another interviewee disagreed, arguing that this is tantamount to dropping "ideological bombs on the lay people" (P10). In his view, people should be taught about nonviolence in more casual and discussion-oriented forums such as Sunday school classes prior to preaching it from the pulpit. While preaching nonviolence is clearly a central practice for nonviolent United Methodists, how one actually goes about doing this is a somewhat murkier enterprise.

Practices of Direct Political Action

A final category of practices includes those that are carried out in the interest of witnessing to God's sovereignty and seeking to transform the wider world and its secular structures of violence. Many participants highlighted practices of direct political action: writing letters to elected officials (P6), withholding taxes used by the government for conducting war (P5), voting (P10), working with legislatures for change (P12), and engaging in nonviolent public protest (P9, P3, P7) sometimes even to the point of arrest (P3). In line with a broader definition of nonviolence as a way of life, some participants named participation with missions such as homeless shelters, soup kitchens, and support groups (P12) as important practices of nonviolence, as is donating money to "worthy causes" (P5).

Involvement with peace organizations (inter-faith, secular, and Christian) was a prominent practice for nonviolent United Methodists; within such organizations opportunities are created for direct action, advocacy, and support (P5, P8, P2, P3). A related practice is that of simple dialogue; "conversation with other peace-loving people" provides opportunity to "listen with a third ear for what's behind this, what's under this" (P6). Such dialogue is usually the conduit for the practice of intentionally searching for "another way to deal" with conflict (P2). Conversation with others creates space to be "creative," to "think outside the box," and to realize "that things are not either/or, black or white, but that there's always a third way, and sometimes a fourth, sixth, twelfth, twenty-ninth way, and to try to look for other explanations or other answers" to war and violence (P6). Suggests another participant: "There's got to be a more excellent way about our learning how to live, and for the large part for all of us, wherever we are, I think it begins with how we negotiate our differences and our hurts and whatever on a personal level; that eventually will make a difference for how people do that on a larger level" (P11).

Finally, a last practice that involves a more public witness is the simple yet often daunting act of speaking up against injustice. Participants recounted stories of confronting injustice in their interpersonal relationships (P2, P10); for one young man, even "objectifying someone is a violent act" (P10) and he has therefore found himself confronting a male friend on occasion when that friend has spoken negatively about women. In their roles as public figures who are involved with church committees and General and Annual Conferences and in leadership in their communities, two pastors have felt the need to be a "pebble in the shoe" (P7) and to speak out "when I think other people are being harmed, whether that is a child in a grocery store getting jerked around, or a person of color being joked about, or a public shaming of somebody else" (P6).

INTERVIEW QUESTION FOUR:

How are United Methodists formed toward nonviolence?

This study seeks to understand how United Methodists arrive at the commitment to nonviolence. In a denomination that does not view nonviolence as a condition of Christian faith nor necessary for church membership, how and why some United Methodists come to view it as central to Christian faith is of particular interest and may shed light on how nonviolence might be seen more readily as a valid Christian response to war and violence. After briefly noting the origins and major influences in individuals' commitments, this section looks more carefully at the role played by the United Methodist Church itself in forming people toward nonviolence.

Origins & Major Influences

When asked about recollections of the first time they learned about nonviolence, many participants recalled being shaped at an early age by key family members. Two participants described their fathers and the influence those relationships had on each of the individuals (P1, P5). Another pointed to an uncle whose experience in World War II and the violence he encountered there led to his anti-war sentiment upon his return home (P11). Others spoke more generally of being raised in a "loving family" (P6) or one in which "problems that we've had with each other get worked out. And so I kind of lived in that environment where you work out your problems with one another and you don't turn your back on someone. You love this person because they're your family member, not because you agree with them, but because they are a person and you were given them in your family and that's what you do. And so I guess kind of growing up in that sort of environment I saw that" (P4).

For others, the commitment to nonviolence grew out of or was at least given a push by some formative experience. This includes pilgrimage to another part of the world such as the Middle East (P1) or South Africa (P6). The attacks on September 11—or more precisely, the United States' response of "rallying to war and mobilizing our military" (P8)—led two young interviewees to adopt an increasingly nonviolent stance (P7, P8). Growing up in the 1960s and "being able to see nonviolence lived out in an intentional way by a large group of people" (P11) was important to two interviewees (P11, P1). One woman pointed to her attendance at a program about nonviolence in parenting entitled "People Are Not for Hitting: Children Are People Too." This led her to begin "looking at retributive justice, and penalizing justice, and restorative justice" (P6). One woman's childhood experiences of fighting on the playground—and often losing those battles—led her at a young age to see violence as a serious evil (P2).

Experiences with Christian faith traditions outside of the United Methodist Church have influenced the development of nonviolent commitments. The example of historic peace churches such as the Mennonite and Quaker traditions is important for some (P1, P6); "I really admire Quakers and Mennonites and people like that who are so staunchly against war that they're willing to go to jail for it and pay a price for it" (P6). Teachings from the Catholic tradition were also influential (P8, P10); one participant claimed that Catholic social teachings had "invaded" his understanding of what it means to be Methodist (P10).

The names of certain people were mentioned several times as being tremendously influential in the development of the nonviolent commitment. The impact of a few theologians at Duke Divinity School would be difficult to question; participants continually referred to the influence of Stanley Hauerwas (P8, P6, P4, P10), Will Willimon (P6, P4, P10) and Peter Storey (P8, P6, P4) on their conceptions and practices of nonviolence. Dr. Martin Luther King, Jr. was, not surprisingly, viewed as a central figure for those who subscribe to a nonviolent outlook (P12, P5, P6, P3, P8, P9, P4).

Though many participants pointed to the impact of John Wesley on their nonviolent commitments, the influence he wields is somewhat more complex. Participants recognized that Wesley was not a pacifist and pointed to his support of violence by the British during the American Revolution (P4, P5, P10); however, Wesley is largely credited as a primary example of how authentic Christianity requires concern for social awareness and activism (P5, P6, P4, P10). For one self-proclaimed "staunch Wesleyan," Wesley's contribution to a discussion about the place of non-violence within Methodism is his emphasis on sanctification. Wesley's influence leads this participant to argue "that the true disciple comes to the point . . . where it's not about making a cognizant choice about every matter in [one's] life, but it becomes a natural state. So, the concept of discipleship, and sanctification, would be a part of this, too, where someone becomes actually nonviolent" (P10). Wesley's influence on another participant's nonviolence is associated with the "open" ecclesiology noted elsewhere in this chapter. For this young pastor, "what keeps me [in the United Methodist Church] is that we can still come to the table, hopefully . . . those who disagree on issues like this can come and can faithfully discuss it. I guess it was Wesley who was credited with saying, 'In essentials unity; in nonessentials liberty; in all things, charity,' and kind of trying to adhere to that sort of thing where . . . in the essentials we're together, and struggling together to work out these issues" (P4).

Nonviolent Formation within the United Methodist Church

This discussion of Wesley's influence carries us into a discussion of the role of the United Methodist Church itself in shaping and sustaining the commitment to nonviolence. Out of twelve interviewees, eleven[4] pointed to specific aspects of the church—whether the United Methodist social witness more generally, the local church or general church upbringing, certain pastors, or education in United Methodist seminaries.

For a majority of participants, caring about social issues and concerns was simply part of the fabric of church life and their participation in it (P1, P2, P3, P6, P7, P9, P10). As one woman who left her Baptist background to join the United Methodist Church put it, "It's just what

4. The nonviolent commitments of the twelfth individual, by inference from the whole of the interview, was also formed at least in part by the United Methodist Church; however, because he did not point to specific aspects of the church that were part of that formation, he is not included with the other eleven.

I've heard people say and do, and the kinds of petitions that go around from the United Methodist Church and some of the organizations in the church all seem to be nonviolent kinds of things, and justice is in the forefront of what they're trying to do" (P2). A woman who grew up in Methodist circles in west Texas said of her church experience: "I would have to say somewhat that it was the water I swam in so I didn't know that it was [focused on social action]" (P6). While nonviolence itself was seldom taught or even mentioned, the broader concern for social issues that was instilled in participants was the seedbed for later developments in the direction of nonviolence. One participant admitted that "it is definitely true that in my home church they don't talk about nonviolence as being something that matters"; despite this reality, "the only thing that I would say is that my upbringing—and I don't think this has much to do with United Methodism as a unique denomination—but my upbringing in the church from birth was incredibly formative to me in a lot of other ways and while it didn't talk about nonviolence, I am sure that I gained values and some sense of who God is. . . . I don't doubt for a minute that my upbringing in the church formed me into the kind of person who could, at a later point and with the right influences, come to understand nonviolence as a central part of the Gospel" (P8).

Pastors have played an important role in some participants' commitments. A participant in his early seventies said that "there were a number of other pastors that I remember hearing as a kid . . . that were close to pacifism, if not actual. So that influenced me as I was growing up." This gentleman is currently a member of a United Methodist congregation where the pastor "is very sympathetic to nonviolence" (P5). When she was in high school, another participant recalled having a pastor who was preaching about peace during the Vietnam War, "and he was getting it in the neck in the local congregation. So, I had a chance to watch him stand up for his commitment, and yet watch people react . . . so I knew at a very young age that standing up for what you believe has a price, and I saw people willing to pay the price" (P1). For one young man, hearing nonviolence preached from the pulpit was highly significant in the development of his nonviolent leanings (P10). These examples seem to confirm one participant's observation that the position of the pastor has much to do with the positions adopted by church members; "you know, in some churches it's very clear, because the pastor has taken a position, and so there's a lot of conversation around [nonviolence]" (P11).

Seminary education is a major factor in forming people toward non-violence as well. One person chose to attend Boston University School of Theology in large part because Walter Mueldar, who was "known for his pacifist stands" (P5), was the dean at that time. The significance of Duke Divinity School has been noted earlier in this section. One Duke graduate and current pastor said: "When I came to divinity school is when a lot of things got really blown wide open because students in my classes had been to Africa, had been on the mission field, had done inner-city ministry, had worked in reconciling work across races, things like that. And so it was sort of like, my goodness, I feel so naïve. I didn't know that Christians were supposed to do those things. I thought that's what Peace Corps people did or something" (P6). Another participant described his seminary-initiated awakening thus:

> And so it wasn't until I got to academic settings and heard guys like Stanley Hauerwas, or Will Willimon, or Peter Storey talking about how . . . the very heart of their faith is the idea of nonviolence. And seeing and hearing these men and women that taught me as well talk about this, and seeing that example, really kind of caused me to say . . . what do I believe and is this something that I feel? It really—when I heard it and began to talk about it, it really struck a chord with me and it felt like something that [was] probably true. And so I started to explore it myself, and to read scriptures, and to prayerfully consider it and felt like this . . . was the way that Jesus taught. This is what we need to be doing or saying. (P4)

And finally, describing it as a less gradual process, one participant explained that nonviolence "was shoved down my throat at Duke. I fought it at first, you know? But it's just what I've become, whether or not I'm actually entirely comfortable with it—actually, I'm not entirely comfortable with it, which I've heard is quite common" (P10).

INTERVIEW QUESTION FIVE:

How do United Methodists view church teachings on war, peace, and nonviolence?

In the textual analysis of United Methodist doctrinal statements conducted in chapter 4, questions were raised about the plurality of doctrinal teachings on issues of war, peace, and nonviolence. Because this study aims to bring these teachings into dialogue with practicing nonviolent

United Methodists, how those individuals view the teachings themselves serves as an important point of departure for the critical dialogue in the following chapter 6.

Views of United Methodist Teachings on War, Peace, and Nonviolence

Study participants had a wide range of views regarding the doctrine of the United Methodist Church on these important issues. One participant thought the Social Principles are potentially a good teaching tool, but personally found them to be "sort of blah" because they try "not to offend too much in any direction" (P5). Several suggested that the Social Principles statements are helpful (P2, P3, P9, P12) and even among "the finest of any denomination" (P12); the problem, however, is that "most United Methodists don't know what the official teachings of the church are" (P3). In the words of one participant, "I think that on paper and doctrinally we are right on target. It's just getting folk to, first of all, even know it. I mean I think that our Social Principles are perhaps the best kept secret from our own church" (P12).

When participants were asked which way they thought the teachings leaned—toward nonviolence or toward a more just war approach—the responses seemed to confirm the sense of confusion that can result from doctrinal plurality, as noted in earlier chapters. One participant simply admitted uncertainly about what the *Book of Discipline* teaches regarding war and nonviolence but said that "if I had to guess I would guess that it is more on the side of nonviolence than most of what's preached. But I would base that on things like the fact that the Council of Bishops is very vocally opposed to this war [in Iraq]. You know, more so than most pastors have" (P8). Three other participants were more certain that the teachings leaned toward nonviolence (P2, P6, P11). One interviewee thought that "officially" the United Methodist Church is a just war church but believes the church is headed in a more nonviolent direction: "I feel quite comfortable with our teachings, because I think that they lean toward nonviolence. I don't think you can argue with our teachings that violence is okay. I really don't think it's possible. Now, we don't flat out accept nonviolence. But I don't think we're pro-violence. We've found some kind of a little island in the midst to step on for a while until we make up our minds" (P10). And one participant was quite sure that just war thinking was the focus of United Methodist teachings on war and nonviolence (P9).

Perhaps of most interest is the division between participants over whether the plurality of views on war and nonviolence contained within the pages of the *Book of Discipline* is a problematic or positive (or at least neutral) feature. Among ten of the 12 interviewees, there was an even split. Five of the participants viewed the doctrinal plurality of views on war and nonviolence as highly problematic. As one participant argued, such plurality becomes a "compromise" which brings the church "very, very close to being lukewarm" (P12); expressing her agreement, another suggested that "we need to take a stand . . . there are some things I think we should not embrace . . . there are too many wiggle points" (P2). Two participants noted other areas in which the United Methodist Church is not clear in its teachings; one stated that "pretty much on every issue, except for gambling, we're a little wish-washy" (P10) and the other noted that "the social principle on divorce could be sketchy also. So I think we have a lot of unclarity" (P7). And one pastor pointed to a more wide-spread confusion: "the pieces that are [in] our *Discipline* are not as clear as the early Christians were about the fact that taking up arms was just not acceptable. So, we have the same kind of confusion, I think, in our denomination that we have in our local churches, amongst our people, that we are not abundantly clear. What is acceptable or not as acceptable? It's okay to pick up arms, it's okay to be in the military, and it's not okay, and it was not okay. So, we do have confusion" (P1).

The other five participants did not view the plurality of stances *necessarily* as a problem. One recognized that one's "experience could be so different, depending on the part of the country you're in" (P3); another pointed to the "different periods in the history of the Methodist Church where we've been more nonviolent and then we've kind of swung back" (P4). One pastor states it eloquently:

> I think that our stance is that we try to support each other in those places where we have convictions, even where we're different, that we try to support each other as individuals . . . you know, sometimes we beat ourselves up for being wish-washy. I think what we do is that we encourage people to think about their response to faith, and although we may not agree with where they end up, acknowledge that we're all growing in who we are, and I still may feel I have the right position, and eventually you'll grow into that place, you know? But that doesn't mean that I need to disassociate with you, or that you need to not be United Methodist . . . it recognizes that

we are growing into the place where God would have us be whole. And so, otherwise we're saying, "Okay, you do this, this, and this, and you're then whole; you're the whole person that God wants you to be." And I don't think that's true. So, there has to be room for that growth, which means we are at different places of development and understanding. That is not to say that that condones violence. You know, it's to say that if we're being violent in whatever way we're being violent, that it means that this is a context for changing, that this is the place to change.... [It's about] embracing the people [without] the positions that they take. And seeing that as a place of hope and growth [and] of transformation—that people can be transformed, and that there are some benchmarks or whatever.... They're not litmus tests. They're signs of change, and that there's an expectation of that, and there's a hope of that. (P11)

Re-writing the Teachings of the United Methodist Church on War, Peace, and Nonviolence

Participants were asked how, if given the opportunity, they would re-write sections of the *Book of Discipline* that deal with these issues. One participant simply wished for a greater theology of sin and confession and "supplication to God for God's mercy that sustains us even in the midst of our sin" (P5). Three participants specifically expressed their desire to see a greater connection to the nonviolent example of Jesus Christ within United Methodist doctrinal teachings (P3, P10, P12). Said one participant, "I would start the statement by saying that as United Methodists, our primary concern is to follow Jesus Christ. That would be exactly how I would describe it and set it up, and from there we can see that Jesus Christ lived a life of nonviolence; therefore, as United Methodists, we must follow the example of Christ, and support, promote, and actively seek nonviolence, or nonviolent ways to be Christians in the world. That's pretty much what I would say" (P10). Another agreed: "I would want to put in information that would help people to make those connections between Scripture, between the life of Jesus, and the current practices, and practitioners of nonviolence.... I think any explicit connection between nonviolence and nonviolent practice and the Christian faith would all be to the point" (P3).

Four participants wished for a greater emphasis on the language of war and violence as "incompatible" with Christian faith, which echoes Article XVI of the Evangelical United Brethren Confession of Faith, as noted in chapter 4 (P8, P3, P6, P4). And half of the participants claimed that if they could re-write the teachings, they would make the church a clearly nonviolent and pacifist church (P1, P2, P7, P9, P11, P12); four of these even wished to align and identify the United Methodist Church with the historic peace churches.

One conversation in particular highlights the complexities and nuances of the issue for nonviolent United Methodists. At first, when asked how he would re-write the *Discipline* to reflect the commitment to nonviolence, one young lay-person said he "would say Christians who are United Methodists ought not to participate in war" but also that churches should support those who "either through conscription or enlistment find themselves" involved in war. The interviewer then asked whether this seemed to be an inconsistent position: "How would you explain that war is incompatible but that the church should support people who do decide to join in . . . the war cause?" The interviewee admitted that this did seem to be an inconsistent position and after further consideration decided that his original answer was in part related to the current debates and questions about how one can be "anti-war and not anti-troop" and the "overarching fear" of being seen by others as unsupportive of U.S. troops in Iraq. In addition, "You've got a situation where probably a substantial majority of American Christians or American United Methodists will feel . . . that the American military has an important duty and role to play . . . so . . . I would want to be sensitive to that in the interest of not just, I guess, alienating or losing a lot of people . . . and probably the fact that . . . as a church we are not willing . . . to go to an extreme like that—that's a reason why we're a large denomination and a reason why we're doctrinally diluted" (P8).

INTERVIEW QUESTION SIX:

How do nonviolent Methodists sustain their commitments to nonviolence in a church that is not nonviolent?

This section delves into how nonviolent United Methodists sustain and negotiate the commitment to nonviolence in a church that is not doctrinally nonviolent. How and why does a person who believes nonviolence is central to Christian faith remain in a denomination that, doctrinally and practically, does not view nonviolence in the same manner? First, however, a look at the tensions that confront nonviolent United Methodists within the church itself demonstrates the degree to which walking the nonviolent path can be treacherous ground for nonviolent Methodists.

Tensions: Nonviolent and United Methodist?

Of twelve interviews with nonviolent United Methodists, only two stated that they had never experienced any form of tension in the church because of their nonviolent positions (P2, P7).[5] One participant who works for a United Methodist-related organization that deals with social concerns pointed to the volume of emails and phone calls she receives that express "outrage" at the organization's position on a number of controversial issues, including war and state-sponsored violence (P3). Two pastors described situations in which a clergy colleague challenged the nonviolent commitment as something less than appropriate to their pastoral leadership (P9, P4). By far the greatest tensions felt by nonviolent United Methodists occurred within the context of worship or a Sunday school class, particularly when the participant preached or taught a nonviolent or anti-war message (P1, P6, P11, P4, P10, P12). While each of the stories that tell of this tension is fascinating in its own right, only one story is highlighted here. It is chosen as an exemplar of the kind of tensions experienced by nonviolent United Methodists because it reveals the various levels and kinds of difficulty to which others point.

Participant 4 ran into difficulty within the first few months of his first pastoral appointment to a small United Methodist congregation in central Pennsylvania. In 2004, he decided to preach a sermon series on the Lord's Prayer; at the adult Sunday school class that followed worship, the class would discuss a corresponding chapter of a book entitled *Lord Teach Us: The Lord's Prayer and the Christian Life.*[6] After only a couple of weeks, a church member who had been most welcoming when the pastor first arrived at the church confronted him about the class, asking if he planned to continue it; the pastor responded in the affirmative. The parishioner arrived at the class that Sunday with a four-page letter in which she accused the pastor of "using this whole study on the Lord's Prayer to push a political agenda" (P4). When she condemned the authors of *Lord*

---

5. One of these two, a pastor from South America who moved to the United States five years ago, did say that she knew of colleagues in other countries who *had* experienced tension between being nonviolent and being Methodist.

6. Willimon and Hauerwas, *Lord Teach Us.*

Teach Us and said she wanted to ban all books written by them, the young pastor reminded her that that was "what the Nazi government did and that's what the Apartheid government did.... These are pretty well-known and respected individuals. Not everyone agrees with them, but you have to be in dialogue with them" (P4). The story continues in the words of the pastor himself:

> And she questioned what I would be preaching, and what I would be teaching. And we have a daycare in our church, and I do have story time with them each week. [And she wanted to know] what would I be reading the kids in the daycare, in the children's moments. And [the authors] allude in the book that maybe dropping atomic bombs wasn't the best idea. And [in this woman's view], to question that decision was un-American and we just shouldn't even be talking about it, we shouldn't be talking about politics in church. And I just was kind of hit, you know, punched in the face. ... But we certainly didn't shut down the class. We continued on. ... Not everyone agreed with everything that these guys were saying, or what I was saying, but most folks valued the discussion. But there were [some] folks ... who did not value the discussion. And it was kind of that idea that you're a Christian here on Sunday mornings, but politics is something different. And ne'er should the two meet. You know, Jesus has nothing to do with—she didn't explicitly say that, but that was kind of the underlying theology, that politics is here, Jesus is here, and there's a wall between the two, a separation of church and state. Don't talk about that. And that kind of amazed me and I was floored.... And so, you know, that ... really hit me hard and it was tough to kind of work through. (P4)

The young pastor later went to a colleague and mentor to tell him about the situation in the church and seek his advice. "And I said, 'We're doing this study on the Lord's Prayer and the authors talk about nonviolence.' And [the colleague's] question was, 'Do you really think you can get nonviolence out of the Lord's Prayer?' And there was no help from him there ... it was pretty much kind of condescending, that I'll grow out of this stage eventually and I'll learn. You know, that's kind of what he said" (P4).

On Leaving the United Methodist Church

Despite challenges such as this to their most central commitments, nonviolent United Methodists express little interest in leaving their church in search of more centrally-nonviolent ecclesial traditions. For a majority of participants, the long Methodist heritage of social concern and activism helps nonviolent people to feel that they have a permanent home in the church (P5, P8, P9, P6, P4, P10, P12). Alongside this factor, two of these participants raised criticisms of the historic peace churches as reason for never having joined one (P5, P8). Some participants expressed the desire and sense of responsibility to work for change in the church from the inside (P2, P3, P8). When asked if she had ever been tempted to leave the United Methodist Church for some other more peace-oriented tradition, one seventy-nine year old participant said that she had not been so tempted and added, "I would like, in whatever tiny way I could, to try to change the Methodist thinking and feeling, rather than leaving, and going to another church" (P2). And one woman, after being asked if she had ever considered leaving the United Methodist Church because it did not consistently agree with her commitments to nonviolence, laughingly said, "No. I think that if I leave the United Methodist Church, I will leave Christianity" (P7).

It is precisely the pluralism of the church that creates space for nonviolent United Methodists to work internally for change in the denomination and to feel that they can find a "niche" (P9) and have a permanent home within the church. Despite holding the "minority position" (P2) when it comes to questions of war and the use of violence, nonviolent United Methodists recognize that "within the Methodist tradition, you can find streams that continue to nourish you and feed you" (P3); in other words, "we are not so rigid, if you will, or structured, that we don't allow for other kinds of experiences to happen in our structure" (P11). As one pastor stated it, "part of what draws me to the United Methodist Church is the breadth of theology and acceptance and diversity in it" (P6). And one pastor drew out both the positive and negative aspects of this pluralism and openness: "one of the strengths of our church and one of the weaknesses of our church is the diversity that we have. It's a strength because we've got this broad umbrella where people can disagree about things but still be part of one community. But it's also a weakness because people look at us and say, 'Well, what do you believe? What do you stand for?' But . . . that's what keeps me there—[it] is that we can still come to the table, hopefully we can. Those who disagree on issues like this can come and can faithfully discuss it" (P4).

CONCLUSION: RESPONSE TO THE CENTRAL
RESEARCH QUESTIONS

Now that the sub-questions which served as the interview questions for the qualitative part of the study have been answered, a summary response can be provided for the first of the central research questions: *What is the lived theology of United Methodist Christians who are committed to nonviolence, and what sustains that commitment?*

The lived theology of nonviolence that arises from this study's qualitative analysis is one that sees nonviolence as central to Christian faith, dynamic and active in its search for effectiveness and practicality, and comprehensive in scope as it reaches into all areas of life. Theologies of nonviolence are deeply rooted in Scripture and theology—particularly to a certain Christocentrism that sees nonviolence as a clear aspect of the teachings and example of Jesus Christ and which calls for following these teachings and example as closely as possible.

In a denomination that does not espouse nonviolence as necessary to Christian faith or to church membership, the commitment to nonviolence is sustained by a few key factors. First, nonviolent United Methodists are sustained by a variety of practices that connect across many different aspects of life and which take on the modifier "nonviolent" because they are named so by nonviolent United Methodists. As Nancy Ammerman argues in *Everyday Religion*, "something becomes religious because it is understood to be so by those who observe and participate in it."[7] While the activities named by participants as practices which exemplify, constitute, and sustain the commitment to nonviolence could in most cases be considered practices which sustain a different position, the practices become practices of nonviolence precisely because nonviolent United Methodists so name them.

Second, the commitment to nonviolence is sustained by the long heritage of social concern and activism within Methodism itself. For many nonviolent United Methodists, the witness of the church on social issues is the seedbed out of which the commitment to nonviolence grows, even despite the fact that most of them did not learn directly from the denomination about nonviolence as a valid option in response to the moral issues of war and violence. It seems to be enough for nonviolent United

---

7. Ammerman, *Everyday Religion*, 224.

Methodists that the wider church should and does care enough to wrestle with moral issues of war and violence.

Finally, for this minority group, the pluralism of the church and the sense of ecclesial openness to dialogue and disagreement is precisely what keeps nonviolent United Methodists from abandoning their church and sustains their commitment to working for change from within the church. For nonviolent United Methodists, this "open" ecclesiology is invaluable in that it recognizes that the church is constituted by fallen people who are in different places in their faith journeys, emphasizes the importance of dialogue and debate, and seeks continual growth in faith and discipleship among its members. For the nonviolent United Methodists interviewed for this study, their current church home—perhaps a bit ironically—is exactly the place where they feel their commitments and lifestyle can thrive. In the following chapter, these findings from the qualitative analysis are brought into dialogue with the doctrinal teachings of the United Methodist Church.

6

Practical-Theological Dialogue

CHAPTER 6 ATTENDS TO practical-theological dialogue between two conversation partners: United Methodist doctrinal teachings related to war and nonviolence and the lived theology of nonviolence as understood and practiced by twelve nonviolent United Methodists. This dialogue more accurately takes the form of a listening session on the part of the doctrine and thereby of the wider denomination. As a minority voice, those who represent the nonviolent commitment in this study are given the opportunity to speak back to their church; the church is asked simply to listen openly to what the lived theology of nonviolence says. In its claims to inclusivity in the United Methodist Church, the *Book of Discipline* states that "an inclusive society is one in which all persons are open, welcoming, fully accepting, and supporting of all other persons, enabling them to participate fully in the life of the church, the community, and the world."[1] In a church that "embraces human beings from a wide variety of groups" and claims that "Only the vows of baptism and Church membership exclude persons" from the ecclesial community,[2] it is important to keep before itself the voice, understanding, experience, and insight of those groups who are fully a part of the Methodist community despite their position as an alternative, minority, or otherwise marginal group.[3]

As noted in chapter 3, existing scholarship on theologies of nonviolence has yet to draw out the beliefs and practices of nonviolence as it is lived out by those who have committed to this way of life. As a research

1. *Book of Discipline* (2004), 93.

2. Jones, *United Methodist Doctrine*, 249.

3. The reader is directed back to the literature reviewed in chapter 3 for scholarship citing the importance of dialogue and listening within the United Methodist Church as well as the reasons why the church need even bother listening to an alternative voice within its ranks.

project which in large part intends to draw out this voice and to facilitate an initial encounter with the current doctrinal teachings of the United Methodist Church, the dialogue evolves in this chapter in an amicable and appreciative manner which seeks to be constructive; findings from the textual analysis and the qualitative interviews demonstrate that the two conversation partners are by no means in complete opposition to one another. In fact, any challenges and promptings that follow in this chapter must be couched in acknowledgment of the tremendous love and appreciation that nonviolent United Methodists have for their church despite the fact that they constitute and hold a minority view within the denomination, at least concerning questions of war and nonviolence. As noted in chapter 5 under "Interview Question Four," a majority of nonviolent United Methodists interviewed for this project perceive their experiences and faith formation in the United Methodist Church to be fundamental to the development of a nonviolent commitment, even if they never heard nonviolence specifically preached from the pulpit or taught in a Sunday school classroom. To repeat one interviewee's words, "I don't doubt for a minute that my upbringing in the church formed me into the kind of person who could, at a later point and with the right influences, come to understand nonviolence as a central part of the Gospel."

The overall purpose of the following critical and constructive dialogue, in line with the goals of Practical Theology outlined in chapter 2,[4] is to help the church better to discern its identity as a church which claims to witness to the story of Jesus Christ. First, in order to lay the foundations for specific challenges to the doctrine and the church by the lived theology of nonviolence, the primary theological grounding of each conversation partner is questioned and assessed in relation to the meaning of "discipleship" as it is defined and described by the *Book of Discipline* itself. Next, findings from the qualitative analysis are brought into dialogue with the doctrinal teachings to see the ways in which the lived theology of nonviolence might challenge the doctrine and the wider United Methodist Church. The dialogue then returns to the question of whether doctrinal pluralism within the United Methodist Church is a source of confusion and therefore a problem, or an appropriate response for an ecclesial body that values freedom of conscience and dialogue about difficult issues.

---

4. See chapter 3 of the study.

Finally, this conversation generates some initial suggestions which point the way toward addressing the conclusions reached in the study.

ASSESSING PRIMARY THEOLOGICAL FOUNDATIONS

The objective in assessing the basic theological foundations of church doctrine and the lived theology of nonviolence, which in part drives the practical-theological findings and conclusions in this chapter, is to understand the theological crux or center of each position and then to weigh the two positions against the meaning of "discipleship" as it is defined by United Methodist doctrine. Prior to this assessment, it is helpful to recall some of the scholarship cited in chapter 3 that outlines major theological differences between just war and nonviolence themselves.

Christian Nonviolence vs. Just War Tradition

In the scholarship cited in chapter 3 under "Distinguishing Positions: Nonviolence and the Just War Tradition," nonviolence is described most often in connection to categories such as discipleship (Allen), what it means to imitate or follow Jesus (Allen, Cahill, Hauerwas, Hehir) and to be in line with the gospel (Fynn, Hehir).[5] In the works cited in the section entitled "Christian Theologies of Nonviolence," Christian nonviolence is almost always tied to biblical accounts of the teachings and example of Jesus Christ (Wink, Yoder, Hauerwas, Sider, Battle, Hays).[6]

On the other hand, scholarly analysis or discussion of just war tradition rarely points to biblical accounts of the teachings and example of Jesus Christ as the foundation of that tradition. In the literature review, Paul Ramsey's work was cited for his insistence that "just-war theory is precisely a theory of statecraft."[7] Just war thinking is not based on a Christocentric foundation or framework to the same extent that Christian nonviolence is; in fact the origins of the just war include pre-Christian

---

5. See chapter 3 of the study. The reader should note that even those who ultimately advocate for a just war position concede that the path of nonviolence is rooted in such categories as discipleship and the imitation of Christ. In fact, James Childress himself argues that "many non-pacifists concede that the dominant tendency of Jesus' life and message is pacifist" (Childress, "Pacifism" in the *Westminster Dictionary of Christian Ethics*, 446).

6. See chapter 3 of the study.

7. Ramsey, *Just War*, 260.

roots in Roman conceptions of justice and political thinking,[8] particularly in the writings of Cicero.[9] Noting various Scripture passages, Robert McAfee Brown argues that

> the overall picture that emerges clearly puts the burden of proof on those who would use Jesus' life or teachings in order to justify going to war. Not only is it wrong to *kill* the enemy—even *hating* the enemy is proscribed. There is a positive command to love the enemy and even to pray for him. He may not be the subject of retaliation; if one is smitten on the cheek, the other cheek must be turned. It is not the warmakers who are blessed, but the peacemakers. . . . The prevailing viewpoint seems clear.[10]

Lisa Cahill agrees, and succinctly: "For those who have carried the Christian moral tradition, then, the question is not whether, all things considered, Jesus represents and calls us to peacemaking (positively) and nonviolence (negatively). That much is established, even in just war thinking from Ambrose and Augustine onward."[11]

However the teachings and example of Christ are certainly not entirely absent from just war thinking. For example, one key teaching of Jesus is an ethic of neighbor love, which is a primary foundation of just war theory.[12] Here the work of Lisa Cahill, which was highlighted in chapter 3, continues to be most helpful for pulling all of these strands together for the purposes of this chapter's practical-theological dialogue. According to Cahill, advocates of nonviolence and just war alike view Scripture as foundational to their respective positions but understand the biblical teachings differently. Those advocating just war acknowledge that the life and teachings of Jesus call the Christian disciple to nonviolence and peace "but they give that mandate less practical force through a process of translation that gives great weight to the social context and more freedom to the biblical and ethical interpreter."[13]

Given the views of the various authors cited above, we might conclude that those who espouse a just war ethic still see biblical accounts of

8. Johnson, "Just War," 328.

9. Long, *Living the Discipline*, 117.

10. Brown, *Religion and Violence*, 17.

11. Cahill, *Love Your Enemies*, 13. Neighbor love is also at the heart of a nonviolent ethic, as the lived theology of nonviolence described in chapter 5 reveals.

12. Ramsey, *War and the Christian Conscience*, xvii.

13. Cahill, *Love Your Enemies*, 12.

Jesus Christ as important to the just war tradition but that such grounding is certainly removed from a clear and unequivocal commitment to a more literal imitation of Christ as the primary source of ethical reflection and decision-making around moral dilemmas of war and violence. The positioning of the teachings and example of Jesus Christ as the center and foundation of ethical thinking around war and violence belongs to the advocate of Christian nonviolence.

Lived Theology

In the lived theology of nonviolence developed in this study, nonviolent United Methodists view the teachings of Jesus Christ as the root and center of the commitment to nonviolence, thereby expressing their agreement and affirmation of the scholarship cited in the literature review. While interviewees point to varying aspects of biblical depictions of Jesus—especially his teachings such as the Sermon on the Mount, his example of non-resistance to his arrest, trial, and crucifixion, and his action for justice throughout his ministry without resorting to violent means—the emphasis on closely following the example of Christ remains central to the commitment to nonviolence. Indeed the lived theology of nonviolence that emerges from discussions with contemporary nonviolent United Methodists is one that recognizes biblical accounts of Jesus' life and teachings as the "canon within the canon."

Such positioning of Jesus Christ as the primary source and norm for Christian ethical thinking has been championed by Christian ethicist Glen Stassen. Stassen argues "for the importance of historically situated, historically particular, concrete ethical norms disclosed in the particular history of Jesus Christ, continuous with the tradition of the Hebrew prophets and especially the prophet Isaiah" and also argues "that Christian discipleship and Christian ethics need those concrete norms."[14] For Stassen,

> Our [Christians'] rejection of provincial narrow-mindedness, racial and nationalistic prejudice, authoritarian dogmatism, and apathetic disengagement—as well as our inclusion of the outcasts, our attention to the voice of the others and the strangers, and our peacemaking affirmation of the valid interests of our adversaries—are not based on our ability to achieve a detached, abstract, ahistorical viewpoint disengaged from our communities. They are

14. Stassen, "Concrete Christological Norms for Transformation," 128.

based on historically particular revelation in a Jew in Galilee, who taught repentance, conversion, faithfulness, love, justice, prayer, mutual servanthood, delivering justice and transforming initiative of peacemaking. . . . It is a mistake for Christians to try to escape historical situatedness by avoiding historical concreteness, or by avoiding the historical, incarnate Jesus.[15]

In other terms, Stassen (along with co-author David Gushee) is convinced "that the moral witness of Jesus Christ our Lord has been neglected, misunderstood and even evaded—not only in Christian ethics as a discipline, but in the general presentation of the Christian faith in thousands upon thousands of churches in our nation and around the world. The result is nothing less than the malformation of Christianity, a faith torn loose from its foundation on the rock of the teachings and example of Jesus Christ."[16]

For theologian Thomas Groome as well, the centrality of the example and teachings of Jesus Christ is central to what it means to live out the Christian story. According to Groome, "Our Story is grounded in historical events and has its highpoint, for Christians, in 'God's historical presence in the life, death, and resurrection of Jesus Christ.' The historical Jesus is the Story Incarnate. True, the written testimonies we have of Jesus were written by post-resurrection communities of faith, but the Christ of faith can never be separated from the Jesus of history. Jesus is the Christ, and the Christ is Jesus of Nazareth."[17] If, as the theologians cited here and in chapter 3 suggest, biblical accounts of Jesus Christ can and should be understood as normative for mainstream Christian ethics and Jesus is central for any contemporary understanding of what it means to *be* a Christian, then the nonviolent commitments of contemporary United Methodists who base those commitments on the person of Jesus deserve consideration by the wider United Methodist Church as an entirely valid and faithful option for those who claim the adjective "Christian."[18] This assertion finds further development later in this chapter.

15. Ibid.

16. Stassen and Gushee, *Kingdom Ethics*, 485.

17. Groome, *Christian Religious Education*, 192–93; the internal quote is from Bernhard W. Anderson, *The Living Word of the Bible* (Philadelphia: Westminster, 1979), 48–61.

18. Importantly, the doctrine of the United Methodist Church—technically, at least—does confirm this assertion. As early as 1968, the church maintained that "nonviolent resistance can be a valid form of Christian witness" and that "in all of these situations members of The Methodist Church have the authority and support of their

Doctrinal Teachings

How does the centrality of the life and teachings of Jesus to the lived theology of nonviolence square with current doctrinal statements[19] about
war, peace, violence, and nonviolence as they are expressed in the Social
Principles statements on "Military Service" and "War and Peace"?[20]

Early within its pages, the *Book of Discipline* claims that the heritage of United Methodism "is grounded in the apostolic witness to Jesus
Christ as Savior and Lord, which is the source and measure of all valid
Christian teachings."[21] Yet within the two Social Principles statements
under consideration, only one explicit reference is made to Jesus Christ;
this occurs in the first line of the statement on "War and Peace," which
echoes the Evangelical United Brethren's Article XVI in asserting that "We
believe war is incompatible with the teachings and example of Christ."
Another sentence rejects conscription as "incompatible with the gospel."
The majority of the wording in each statement, however, seems to express
an ethic that is not necessarily based in Christian theological understanding but that could apply to secular institutions as well. This is evident
in language that accepts the implementation of war and violence when
"peaceful alternatives have failed" and "only in extreme situations." Issues
such as individual conscience, the rule of law in international disputes,
and the need for demilitarization are couched in language that could easily be utilized by almost any secular organization or institution to teach
about war and violence.

Church (*Discipline* 1968, 60)." And the most recent doctrinal affirmations of the United
Methodist Church by no means forbid members from adopting a nonviolent lifestyle
and commitment and in fact claim even to "honor the witness of pacifists" within the
denomination (*Book of Discipline* [2004], 122). The problem lies in 1) how to interpret
the plurality of doctrinal views on the topic of war and peace and 2) the church's claim
squared against how the church has (or has *not*) tangibly honored and supported the
nonviolent witness.

19. That is, the statements on war and peace that are part of the most recent (2004)
Book of Discipline.

20. For the sake of manageability, only the two Social Principles statements are
assessed here. Article XVI of the Evangelical United Brethren's Confession of Faith is
described in further detail in chapter 4 and will not be re-examined here. Because the
Resolutions are understood as "amplifications" of the Social Principles statements contained in the *Book of Discipline*, the Resolutions highlighted in chapter 4 also will not be
re-examined here.

21. *Book of Discipline* (2004), 41–42.

As official doctrinal pronouncements set forth by an ecclesial body that posits Jesus Christ as the "source and measure" of all valid teachings, the fact that the Social Principles statements on war, peace, and violence lack any explicit grounding in specific teachings of Jesus Christ is a serious deficiency. In comparing the lived theology of nonviolence that arises from this study's qualitative interviews with the teachings of the Social Principles of the United Methodist Church, it is clear that nonviolent Methodists place a much more explicit value on biblical accounts of Jesus Christ as normative for thinking ethically about war and peace and for their interpretation of what it means to live the Christian life.

The Meaning of "Discipleship" in the United Methodist Church

Scholarship cited in chapter 3 pointed to the centrality of the teachings and example of Jesus Christ in the development of a theology of non-violence. Additional scholarship introduced in the current chapter points to the normativity of Christ's teachings for ethics more generally and particularly in the call to authentic Christian discipleship. A look at the understanding of Christian discipleship as defined within the *Discipline* itself is an important next step in the practical-theological conversation unfolding in the current chapter.

Within the pages of the *United Methodist Book of Discipline*, there are several clear statements about how "discipleship" is defined and understood. According to the General Rule of Discipleship, discipleship means "To witness to Jesus Christ in the world, and to follow his teachings through acts of compassion, justice, worship, and devotion. . . ."[22] Elsewhere, the *Discipline* argues for "the identification of church membership with discipleship to Jesus Christ."[23] In Part III of the *Discipline*, "The Ministry of All Christians," the claim is made that "the ministry of all Christians is *shaped by the teachings of Jesus* [italics mine]. The handing on of these teachings is entrusted to leaders who are gifted and called by God to appointed offices in the church: some apostles, some prophets, some evangelists, some pastors and teachers, to equip the saints for the work of ministry, for the building up of the body of Christ (Ephesians 4:11–12). For these persons to lead the church effectively, they must *embody the teachings of Jesus* in servant ministries and

22. *Book of Discipline* (2004), 552–53.
23. Ibid., 516.

servant leadership [italics mine]."[24] These passages make clear the connections—according to the *Discipline* itself—between discipleship and a close following of the teachings of Jesus.

An important aspect of this discussion is a statement within the *Discipline* that calls upon each member "to be a witness for Christ in the world, a light and leaven in society, and a reconciler in a culture of conflict" and "to identify with the agony and suffering of the world and to radiate and exemplify the Christ of hope." The *Discipline* goes on to assert that "The standards of attitude and conduct set forth in the Social Principles (Part IV) shall be considered as an essential resource for guiding each member of the Church in being a servant of Christ on mission."[25] One can see the problem and failed system that is disclosed once all of the pieces are put together: the doctrine of the church itself claims that discipleship is about following the teachings of Jesus Christ; the Social Principles statements on war and peace do not clearly reflect a specific and explicit rootedness in the teachings of Jesus Christ; yet the church encourages people to use the Social Principles as "standards of attitude and conduct" to guide church members to be more like Jesus Christ. How can teachings which do not explicitly rely on and reflect the teachings of Jesus help United Methodists to become better Christian disciples?

Thus far, the following important points have been established: 1) Christian nonviolence is more explicitly rooted in literal understandings of what it means to follow the teachings and example of Jesus Christ than is the just war tradition; 2) the lived theology of nonviolence, which is grounded in the teachings of Jesus Christ, has validity based on the criteria for valid Christian teachings set forth by the church itself; and 3) the United Methodist Church explicitly connects discipleship to following the teachings of Christ. A logical argument can thus be made that, according to the doctrine of the church itself, the way of nonviolence is a more authentic expression of Christian discipleship than the vision set forth by the current doctrinal statements that address war, peace, and nonviolence. These conclusions prepare the way for specific challenges to the doctrine and to the wider United Methodist Church by the lived theology of nonviolence.

24. Ibid., 91.
25. Ibid., 138.

CHALLENGES TO THE CHURCH FROM A NONVIOLENT PERSPECTIVE

Given the line of argument constructed thus far, the lived theology of nonviolence arising from the qualitative aspect of this study poses many questions and insights to both the doctrine of the United Methodist Church and to the wider denomination. A few of the most prominent include challenges to particular wording in the two Social Principles statements; broader questions of authentic discipleship, including how such discipleship interprets Jesus Christ and his teachings and promotes the call to prophetic witness in and by the church; and practical concerns about how the United Methodist Church does or does not actually honor and support those members for whom nonviolence is central to Christian faith.

Doctrinal Wording

The first challenge to take up is one of wording in current Social Principles statements on war and nonviolence. In the most current version of the statement on "Military Service," the last sentence reads thus: "As Christians we are aware that neither the way of military action, nor the way of inaction is always righteous before God." This sentence implies that in a difficult situation that may call for intervention, only two options are available: military (presumably violent) intervention or no response at all. The lived theology of nonviolent United Methodists strongly challenges the notion that the alternative to violence is "inaction" or doing nothing. As described in the qualitative analysis in chapter 5, inaction in the face of injustice and oppression is hardly a category for those who define themselves as nonviolent. In fact, as noted earlier some Methodists adopt nonviolence at least in part because of its utility—in other words, precisely because they believe it to be *more effective than* war and violence for pursuing and achieving lasting justice and peace.

It is crucial that United Methodist doctrine reflect more truthfully the depth and richness of nonviolent belief and practice, instead of aligning it incorrectly with "the way of inaction." The equation of nonviolence, as it is defined by nonviolent United Methodists, with "doing nothing" reinforces the idea that there is no third option available to the Christian—an option which attempts to follow the teachings and example of Christ by avoiding violence while still emphasizing and displaying a profound commitment to justice, love of neighbor, and compassion by confronting injustice and oppression directly, just not violently. In line with one study participant's comments that, "I don't think we've got much [in the doctrine] that points to a broad and deep understanding of nonviolence" which "would help people to make those connections between Scripture, the life of Jesus, and current practices" (P3), at the very least the doctrine of the church must contain a more nuanced and developed sense of what active nonviolence might look like, rather than linking it falsely to an image of indifference, complacency, and detachment as other people in the world are brutalized and oppressed.

An issue with wording exists in the statement on "War and Peace" as well; this issue was raised earlier in the dissertation and is noted again although briefly here. The first sentence in the statement echoes the Evangelical United Brethren's Article XVI in its claim that "We believe war is incompatible with the teachings and example of Christ." Homosexuality is also defined as "incompatible" with Christian teaching. A tremendous doctrinal and practical inconsistency exists within a church that labels two things in exactly the same condemnatory way but then takes strict action on only one of them. Either war *and* homosexuality both are not actually incompatible with the teachings of Christ or war *and* homosexuality are both incompatible with those teachings. It seems there are only two options to remedy this glaring inconsistency if the language of "incompatibility" around both issues is to be kept: either to discontinue the practice of removing practicing homosexuals from their clergy positions or to begin the practice of removing from the pulpit any pastor who verbalizes her or his support of a given war.

One might argue that this is little more than a fussy spat over semantics—and that few people actually read the *Book of Discipline* for guidance on ethical issues anyway. However as Thomas Frank argues, "it must be taken with utmost seriousness, not just because it is the book of church law, but because it is the record of practices the church intends. It is a book of accountability for the discipline United Methodists profess. It provides the structures and procedures that can put that discipline into practice."[26] Furthermore, asserts Scott Jones, "the denomination ought to give more attention to the clarity of its teaching. There is a sense in which such unanswered questions are problematic if the Church really

---

26. Frank, *Polity, Practice, and the Mission of the United Methodist Church*, 114.

does believe its doctrine is important."[27] Unless written doctrine is intended *purposely* to be meaningless for the church and for the world to which it ministers, what church statements actually say is tremendously important. Otherwise, there is simply no point to having doctrine in the first place and the United Methodist Church might just as well destroy the *Discipline.* But the church does, after all, affirm the *Book of Discipline* as its "book of law." Internal inconsistency in a system of law results in incoherence in trying to follow that law: individuals will do as they please and point to the specific part of the law that best suits their actions and beliefs. Perhaps worse, and as the issue of homosexuality in the United Methodist Church demonstrates, internal inconsistency creates a situation in which arbitrarily-chosen issues can be enforced while others can be entirely ignored.[28] At the very moment that one refers to doctrinal statements within this "book of law" to oust a homosexual pastor from her pulpit, it becomes a tool of reckoning. Such arbitrary and illogical picking and choosing of certain issues for enforcement is a critical shortcoming within United Methodism.

Discipleship

A second challenge posed by the perspective of nonviolent Methodists concerns wider questions of authentic discipleship to Christ and of the role of prophetic witness by the church. In a previous section, an understanding of discipleship was set forth based on teachings found within the *United Methodist Book of Discipline* itself and a claim was made that the explicit concern of nonviolent United Methodists to follow quite literally the teachings of Christ presented a stronger and more accurate vision of discipleship than that presented by current wording in the Social Principles statements related to war, peace, and nonviolence.

In the lived theology of nonviolence described by nonviolent United Methodists, one notices that this minority group is clear in its quest for a more vigorous discipleship to Christ. The collective sense of being on an intentional path toward becoming more like Jesus Christ is a powerful witness to the church. That witness calls, challenges, and encourages

27. Jones, *United Methodist Doctrine,* 57.

28. I am grateful to Glen Messer, Th.D., for his insights regarding the problems inherent in doctrinal inconsistency in the United Methodist Church.

others within the denomination to greater and more faithful discipleship to Jesus of Nazareth, the Christ of faith.

A brief look at literature on this topic shapes further discussion of discipleship. Particularly as understandings of discipleship relate to ethical questions of war and peace, recent works by Glen Stassen and Robert Brimlow offer important insights. Glen Stassen laments the state of most Christian ethical reflection in the twentieth century, which "avoided extensive reference to Jesus' teachings. It frequently defined Christian living in abstract terms such as love or forgiveness, not on the basis of careful biblical exegesis but according to the dominant secular theories of the day."[29] Stassen argues for discipleship based on an "incarnational" ethic in which Jesus Christ is the norm and center of ethical reasoning:

> Discipleship is based on an embodied or incarnational Christology, a view of Christ as representing a specific and concrete alternative way of life meant to be followed. We advocate an embodied Christology which is an alternative to views of Christ that, though they make Godlike claims for the Savior, fail to see Christ's way as the authoritative model for our ethical practice. We advocate Christologies that a) see Christ as divine Sovereign of all of life, not only Sovereign over a "separate" sphere of life (the spiritual); b) define the meaning of Christ in terms that include faithfully following Christ now; c) interpret Jesus' teachings as related to concrete practices that can guide us to live in the real world, not merely as high and abstract ideals; and d) are attentive to Jesus' humanity as one who modeled a way of life to be followed and saw himself as fulfilling the tradition of the Law and the Prophets, not a Constantinian tradition of alignment with political and economic power. We want to build our peacemaking on a Christology that stays close to the Jewish servant Lord of the Gospels who called his disciples humbly to follow his way of nonviolent love, community-restoring justice, and peacemaking initiatives.[30]

Importantly, this view of discipleship as Christ's reign over all of life connects to the characteristic of nonviolence as comprehensive and concerned with all areas of life, as expressed in the lived theology of nonviolence presented in chapter 5. This too challenges the church by encouraging it to

---

29. Stassen, *Living the Sermon on the Mount*, 196.

30. Stassen, *Just Peacemaking*, 6–7. Also Stassen, *Living the Sermon on the Mount*, 195–96.

look at Christ's lordship over all of life instead of compartmentalizing and limiting that lordship by applying it arbitrarily to certain parts of life only.

Robert Brimlow relates the concept of Christian discipleship to ethical reflection on violence and nonviolence as well: "At the risk of putting it too negatively, part of what is entailed by our call to follow Jesus is that we are called away from violence. We are not called to be pacifists; we are called to be Christians, and part of what it means to be Christian is to be peacemakers."[31] Further on, Brimlow draws out the ramifications of radical discipleship to Christ's teachings, wrestling on a very personal level with the difficulties of such a stance despite the strength of his convictions. The entirety of his seventh chapter, "The Christian Response" to the question of what to have done about Hitler is recorded here:

> At this juncture it is time for me to respond to the Hitler question: how should Christians respond to the kind of evil Hitler represents if just war theory and supreme emergencies are precluded, and if we live with a different meaning of success?
>
> We must live faithfully; we must be humble in our faith and truthful in what we say and do; we must repay evil with good; and we must be peacemakers. This may also mean as a result that the evildoers will kills us. Then, we shall also die.
>
> That's it. There is nothing else—or rather, anything else is only a footnote to this. We are called to live the kingdom as he proclaimed it and be his disciples, come what may. We are, in his words, flowers flourishing and growing wild today, and tomorrow destined for the furnace. We are God's people, living by faith.
>
> The gospel is clear and simple, and I know what the response to the Hitler question must be. And I desperately want to avoid this conclusion. When my time comes, I may well trot out every nuanced argument I can develop, or seek a way out in St. Thomas Aquinas or Paul Ramsey. This would serve me and my fear, my hypocrisy, and my faithfulness very well. But I would not be telling the truth or living as I ought and as I am called to live.[32]

These conceptions of discipleship are supported by scholarship that is carried out from a Methodist perspective and which therefore provides some insight on the topic specific to United Methodist doctrine, polity, ecclesiology, and witness. William Willimon echoes Brimlow's thoughts on the difficult and inherently radical nature of discipleship in his assess-

31. Brimlow, *What about Hitler?*, 11.
32. Ibid., 151.

ment that "The way Jesus invites us to walk is a narrow way, so against the stream, so uncommon that anything less than intentional, careful, Christian formation will not do.... From all that we know of Jesus and his demands upon us, being a disciple of his is a good deal more demanding than the completion of a pledge card and the right hand of fellowship. Discipleship requires a lifetime of commitment, trial and error, struggle, correction, prayer, and a host of virtues which cannot be had simply by wanting them."[33]

The Methodist scholars Rieger and Vincent posit the teachings and example of Jesus Christ as normative for Christian ethics and discipleship in their understanding of discipleship as "the actual experimental practice of Christlikeness in the world of people and politics" and argue that it is connected to a "spirituality of radical adherence to the model of Christ" which results in "inward transformation."[34] Finally, the views of Stanley Hauerwas around the centrality of the Jesus of the Gospels align with but also move beyond Stassen's thoughts on discipleship. For Hauerwas, "We are called to be like God: perfect as God is perfect. It is a perfection that comes by learning to follow and be like this man whom God has sent to be our forerunner in the kingdom. That is why Christian ethics is not first of all an ethics of principles, laws, or values, but an ethic that demands we attend to the life of a particular individual: Jesus of Nazareth."[35] Furthermore, "to be like Jesus is to join him in the journey through which we are trained to be a people capable of claiming citizenship in God's kingdom of nonviolent love—a love that would overcome the powers of this world, not through coercion and force, but through the power of this one man's death."[36]

In the previous section, discipleship as it is understood within the pages of the *Book of Discipline* was defined. While these doctrinal understandings of discipleship rightly point to the teachings of Jesus and the importance of following those teachings, the lived theology of nonviolence amplifies and fills out this understanding by affirming nonviolence as a sure aspect of biblical accounts of the life and teachings of Jesus. The literature introduced above serves to support the interpreta-

33. Willimon, *Why I Am a United Methodist*, 48.
34. Rieger and Vincent, *Methodist and Radical*, 39.
35. Hauerwas, "Jesus and the Social Embodiment of the Peaceable Kingdom," 121.
36. Ibid., 121.

tions by study participants that nonviolent practice and commitment is indeed necessary to and for authentic and mature Christian discipleship. This model of discipleship challenges others in the church to see the example and teachings of Jesus Christ as the primary model for Christian belief and behavior.

The Prophetic Witness

As was discussed in chapter 5, study participants relayed numerous stories and experiences which help to draw out the connection between discipleship (understood as following the teachings of Jesus Christ) and the related consequence of sometimes having to take a prophetic stance when pushing for nonviolent theology and practice. Abraham Heschel describes the notion of prophecy in part as "a way of thinking as well as a way of living"[37] and explains that the role of the prophet is "not only to upbraid, but also to 'strengthen the weak hands and make firm the feeble knees' (Isa.35:3). Almost every prophet brings consolation, promise, and the hope of reconciliation along with censure and castigation. . . . His essential task is to declare the word of God to the here and now."[38] Additionally Walter Brueggeman argues: "The task of prophetic ministry is to nurture, nourish, and evoke a consciousness and perception alternative to the consciousness and perception of the dominant culture around us."[39] To act prophetically means not only to criticize the "dominant consciousness" and the surrounding culture but to provide an alternative way of living through an "alternative community."[40] These notions of the prophetic lend a broad definition of what it means for the church to be prophetic: "the church is fulfilling its prophetic function when it is spotlighting injustices in our society, speaking truth to power, proposing specific alternatives, and attempting to alter basic social policy."[41] In addition, the church is acting prophetically when "it takes seriously Jesus' call to be salt and light in the world and it is willing to take action to root out those ills which are the cause of misery for so many."[42] Finally, the prophetic witness is also

37. Heschel, *Prophets*, 1:xiv.

38. Ibid., 12.

39. Brueggemann, *Prophetic Imagination*, 13.

40. Ibid., 13–14.

41. Corbett and Smith, *Becoming a Prophetic Community*, 28.

42. Moore, *A Church to Believe In*, 136–37.

linked to imitation of Christ as discipleship; as one scholar describes the prophetic life, "To live for Christ means to be a living Christ-sign. It is to reflect the image of Christ; it is to be a living letter of Christ. It is living a prophetic life."[43] If nonviolence is at the heart of Jesus' ministry on earth, as study participants and so many theologies of Christian nonviolence cited in this study assert, then living nonviolently in a violent world means living prophetically.

While the *Discipline* claims that the Social Principles "are a call to faithfulness and are intended to be instructive and persuasive in the best of the prophetic spirit,"[44] the doctrine fails to provide any developed description of what this might mean or of what is meant more generally by this use of the word "prophetic."[45] For Methodist scholar Scott Jones, lack of doctrinal clarity is a key aspect of the church's inability to have a serious prophetic witness: "The vitality of the Church's witness depends on the clarity of the Church's teachings . . . ."[46] Further on Jones asserts: "Giving the best possible answer [to questions of what the United Methodist Church believes] empowers the Church's witness. Filling these holes would improve the denomination's proclamation."[47]

Continual movement toward following Jesus Christ will call for a greater willingness to speak and act prophetically in a world that does not recognize Jesus Christ. Growth in discipleship means that, like the nonviolent United Methodists interviewed for this project, there will likely be a direct correlation between the increasing tension one feels between the ways of Christ and the ways of the world and the decreasing level to

43. Buthelezi, "Church as a Prophetic Sign," 141.

44. *Book of Discipline* (2004), 95.

45. Some references to the "witness" of the church, however, were found and are notable given this chapter's discussion. The 1972 *Book of Resolutions* states: "The tradition of nonviolent love is a fundamental dimension of the Christian faith. Christians are challenged to consider and embrace this personal stance, thus providing a redemptive witness in society" (*Book of Resolutions* [1972], 15). Here the language seems almost to equate the witness of the church with a nonviolent stance. And the 2004 *Book of Resolutions* contains a resolution which calls for a program on "ministry training and consultation on social witness" for Native American congregations. "Such a program will be designed and patterned after the gospel of Jesus Christ, which will empower congregations to engage in social witness to their respective Native American communities" (*Book of Resolutions* [2004], 369). Here an explicit connection is drawn between the gospel of Jesus Christ and the social witness of the church in its community.

46. Jones, *United Methodist Doctrine*, 28–29.

47. Ibid., 57.

which one is comfortable with how the world goes about conducting its "business as usual." Speaking and acting prophetically might mean losing allies, facing persecution, and even living dangerously close to death.[48] Yet the community of faith is called to this over and against bending to worldly ways when those ways contradict what the disciple believes to be the way of authentic faith. The prophetic witness of nonviolent United Methodists—and the faith required to speak for what is believed to be true and right despite the risks—presents a challenge to the church which pushes it toward a more costly discipleship and therefore toward a stronger counter-cultural witness.

Supporting the Nonviolent Commitment

Finally, the experiences of nonviolent United Methodists raise practical concerns about how the church supports (or fails to support) those who commit to nonviolence. While research participants pointed to their church experience as the catalyst for their social concern and activism and the seedbed out of which the commitment to nonviolence would eventually grow, the majority did not learn of nonviolence as a "fundamental dimension of the Christian faith"[49] despite the fact that "[i]t is the responsibility of the Church at all levels to inform its members of the fact that conscientious objection, as well as conscientious participation, is a valid option for Christians."[50] A study by Methodist theologian and pastor S. Ronald Parks lends support to the claim arising from the lived theology of nonviolence that the United Methodist Church does not sufficiently support the nonviolent ethic. In his case study of Methodist conscientious objectors during the Vietnam War, Parks argues that the Methodist conscientious objector adopted "a position that the majority of Methodists have valued but not supported."[51] Furthermore, concludes Parks, "Support for the pacifist minority has been expressed in the official pronouncements of the church but seldom promoted by the programmatic agencies

48. Buthelezi, "Church as a Prophetic Sign," 142. Buthelezi suggests that "The highest form of prophetic witness is when the prophet declares the divine message not just in words but through the substance of his body. That happens when the prophet is placed in a position of dying for the sake of the message. Resurrection as was the case with Christ is the vindication of prophetic witness through death."

49. *Book of Resolutions* (1972), 15.

50. *Book of Resolutions* (1980), 38.

51. Parks, "Free (but Not Helped) to Be Pacifist," 204.

of the denomination."[52] If the nonviolent ethic is not only a valid but also deeply faithful option for United Methodists, then the church must make a greater effort to provide education about this option and support for those who adopt it.

These are just a few of the challenges presented to the doctrine of the United Methodist Church and to the wider denomination itself by the lived theology of nonviolence expressed by study participants. Some practical suggestions for beginning to address these challenges are provided in this chapter's concluding section. First, however, the dialogue returns to the question of doctrinal plurality raised earlier in the dissertation; addressing this question draws the lived theology and the doctrinal teaching into further dialogue.

DOCTRINAL CONFUSION OR APPROPRIATE INCLUSION?: ECCLESIOLOGICAL[53] CONSIDERATIONS

Important questions were raised in chapter 4 regarding whether current teachings on war and nonviolence in United Methodism are a source of confusion in the church or an appropriate reflection of an open and inclusive ecclesiological heritage. As noted in previous chapters, some scholars have pointed to the inherent problems of doctrinal pluralism generally (chapter 3) and others have pointed to the confusion generated by the plurality of views on war and nonviolence in particular (chapters 3 and 4). On the other hand, a number of scholars have highlighted the "inclusiveness"[54] of the church and the openness to dialogue and disagreement as important aspects of the Methodist heritage (chapter 3).

How do nonviolent United Methodists weigh in on the question of "confusion or inclusion"? As demonstrated in chapter 5 of the dissertation, nonviolent United Methodists affirm the value of a church that is welcoming of their firmly-held commitments to nonviolence despite the church's doctrinal leanings in the direction of just war thinking. For the most part, nonviolent United Methodists do not want to establish nonviolence as a requirement of membership or inclusion, which would work

52. Ibid., 214.

53. Any discussion of United Methodist ecclesiology must begin with the disclaimer that "One of the least well-defined areas of United Methodist doctrine is its ecclesiology" (Jones, *United Methodist Doctrine*, 246). There exists a remarkable lack of scholarship on the topic, making it difficult to define and characterize a Methodist ecclesiology.

54. Ibid., 248.

directly against the Methodist heritage of "open inquiry." What nonviolent United Methodists do express is a desire for better theological grounding within the doctrinal teachings on issues of war and nonviolence and more tangible and practical support for a lifestyle and commitment that the United Methodist Church itself claims is fully valid and faithful. In short, the lived theology of nonviolence presented in chapter 5 affirms an open and inclusive ecclesiology of the church but asks for greater endorsement and for more substantial support of their nonviolent commitments.

This discussion of openness to dialogue and disagreement, along with the value such openness is given by nonviolent United Methodists who hold this minority view, reveals a level of inconsistency on the part of some of this study's interviewee-participants. Two participants who made explicit reference to their appreciation of an open denomination and doctrine that allow space for many different views later expressed a desire, if it were left to them to do so, to re-write the doctrinal teachings of the church in a way that would make the church sweepingly pacifist. But other participants seem to feel that removing other positions on war and violence as options for United Methodist Christians would in effect create a situation in which those who disagree with the doctrine could potentially be suppressed or even ousted from the church. Such treatment of those who hold the minority view is precisely what nonviolent United Methodists, as the current minority on the issue of war and violence, would not want to see happen, especially since the lived theology of nonviolence described here emphasizes an ecclesiology that places more value on staying together through and despite difficult times than on some kind of doctrinal-ethical purity.

What are the implications of "open inquiry" and "doctrinal pluralism" within Methodist ecclesiology? Despite affirmation by nonviolent United Methodists, openness and plurality present some very difficult questions for the church. Some of the implications of doctrinal pluralism (related to "law" and internal inconsistency) were addressed earlier in the chapter. In addition, the hodgepodge of teachings on war and peace means that church members can avoid confrontation over difficult moral issues; instead, statements that reflect a specific viewpoint can simply be inserted, making it possible to justify a given position without having to arrive at any kind of consensus. The question then remains: which position or side is "right," or at least "more right"? Which position exhibits deeper faithfulness? How can the church pass firm judgments on a complicated moral issue when it seems that every position on that moral issue has been affirmed within the doctrine?

In terms of ecclesial openness, related questions arise. What are the limits of ecclesial openness? What persons (representing which views) should be included and should anyone (and their respective views) be excluded? Openness cannot mean that an absolute free-for-all would be acceptable; otherwise United Methodism loses any identity and center that it might have in the first place. An absolute openness can lead to a kind of "cheap" inclusion which makes no demands of those who are included; this in turn leads to a church characterized by a lack of identity and centered-ness, which leads to apathy and eventually to dissolution. While he does not paint such a dire picture as this study's author, Methodist theologian Thomas Frank points to some of the important questions that arise from ecclesial openness. Pointing to the "continuing vitality of caucuses," Frank asserts that "General Conference has become an enormous experiment in Christian community. How can a conference of a thousand people from over twenty nations create unity out of their diverse needs, interests, and perspectives? . . . How can divergent opinions be heard and acknowledged even as the conference votes on issues? Is there a way to avoid creating "winners" and "losers"? Can General Conference still reflect the consensus or "mind of the church" on important matters? . . . The General Conference lives through these and like questions every time it gathers."[55]

How then might the insights of the lived theology of nonviolence speak to these problems? How can we attend both to the affirmation of ecclesial openness and doctrinal plurality and to the problems and questions inherent in that openness and plurality? One way to address this is to suggest that *ecclesial inclusivity only "works" within the context of a church that is serious about the call to discipleship.*

To state it another way: the values of ecclesial openness include welcoming different views, being open to dialogue and disagreement, and affirming people at different stages of the journey or process of Christian faith. If people are welcomed in as they are but are never challenged or encouraged or formed into something more, then the church is likely to look like little more than any social club. However, if the call to serious discipleship is set alongside or squared with an ecclesial openness which

---

55. Frank, *Polity, Practice, and the Mission of the United Methodist Church,* 267–68.

welcomes differing views *but also* sees the tremendous importance of transformation toward ever-increasing faithfulness and discipleship to Jesus Christ, ecclesial chaos might possibly be avoided. Ecclesial openness allows the church to embrace people from all walks of life who are at various stages of faith; however, a serious commitment on the part of the church to "making disciples" means that as time passes, the individual who was welcomed into the life of the church will become a significantly different person—more like a disciple of Christ—from the person she was when she first joined the community.

As this relates to questions of war, peace, and nonviolence, a lived theology of nonviolence would ultimately say that even given its assertion that nonviolence is central to a mature Christian faith, people who do not hold a commitment to nonviolence should certainly be embraced by the church as full and participating members of the community, whose views and beliefs must be heard and attended to; in this way they affirm Thomas Frank's assertion that "the [United Methodist Church] is structured first and foremost for mission. By tradition and polity it is set up to invite people to Christian faith and life, to provide them the disciplines of Christian discipleship, and to send them into their communities as catalysts of a loving and just society."[56] But also in line with Frank, the lived theology of nonviolence posits an ongoing movement toward being more like Jesus Christ which, again, is the basis for a United Methodist understanding of discipleship. As individuals are formed to be more like Christ, they should likely become increasingly nonviolent at the same time that they become increasingly concerned for justice and compassion in the world. The lived theology of nonviolence holds that the invitational, inclusive, and open ecclesiology of the United Methodist Church can and should be affirmed, so long as the church is willing and able to be entirely intentional about calling people to discipleship to Christ—a discipleship which includes living nonviolently. As Lisa Cahill declares: "The engendering moment of Christian pacifism is the simple conviction that violence is just not consistent with the sort of person Jesus is or the life he lived, a life the discipleship community shares. Jesus' mercy, forgiveness, and compassion are like God's, and the Christian is incorporated into his life. To be a Christian means seriously and actually to live like Jesus."[57]

---

56. Ibid., 34.

57. Cahill, *Love Your Enemies*, 233.

OPEN ECCLESIOLOGY AND SERIOUS DISCIPLESHIP: IMPLICATIONS FOR THE CHURCH

Based on the lived theology and doctrinal affirmations of an open ecclesiology and the assertion of nonviolence as a certain aspect of authentic discipleship, let us imagine what this might mean for the United Methodist Church—and what it might look like for the church to make a turn toward more energetically affirming an ethic of nonviolence. The purpose of the following section is to deal with some of the implications of conclusions drawn in the practical-theological dialogue above.

One implication involves the relationship between ecclesiology and ethics, particularly as the just war and nonviolent positions have been related to a particular ecclesiology by some scholars. As J. Bryan Hehir has argued, "the pacifist position has historically been related to a conception of the Church which Troeltsch and others have designated as sectarian. The term implies that the ethics of discipleship and the obligations of citizenship are normally in tension and often in opposition. The sectarian position has been most clearly exemplified in the peace churches where the ethical imperative of pacifism has produced an ecclesiological position."[58] On the other hand, "the just-war ethic has been tied, theologically and historically," to a different ecclesiological stance: namely, one that "assumes that the Church has a positive responsibility to participate in the process of building a more just and peaceful human society."[59] In reference to the United Methodist Church in particular, Frank hints at the relationship between ecclesiology and ethics in his assertion that

> the [United Methodist Church's] judgment on social issues has been addressed not so much to church members, but to the larger society or government. This mirrors an assumption . . . that United Methodism is influential in American society, that the public and particularly public officials care about the church's stand. The issue today is whether the real challenge to the church is in trying to influence the larger society, or in developing patterns of disci-

58. Hehir, "Just-War Ethic," 32–33. Hehir draws into his arguments the work of Hauerwas, *Vision and Virtue: Essays in Christian Ethical Reflection.*

59. Hehir, "Just-War Ethic," 33. Also Johnson, "Just War," 328: "The historical context of [just war] reasoning was provided by the perceived need for Christians to participate in defending the Roman Empire, by that time a Christian state, from invading Germanic peoples. Just war tradition in Christian thought thus historically came into being as a product of a close relation between church and secular society, and it has ever since developed in dialogue with the requirements of statecraft as manifested in different areas."

plined formation in which its own members model the just society envisioned by the church—or both.[60]

The lived theology of nonviolence seems to defy such tidy links between nonviolence and a "sectarian" ecclesiology and between a just war ethic and a more "public" ecclesiology; nonviolent United Methodists are clear in their assertions that nonviolence calls for active engagement in and with societal and political structures in order to affect change. Still, clarification of Methodist ecclesiology—specifically in reference to questions regarding for whom and for what purpose the church exists—is important for the church as it continues to wrestle with appropriate responses to questions of war and violence. Further development of a nonviolent ethic in relation to its ecclesiology would have implications for the church's ethical deliberations on other moral issues as well. Nonviolent United Methodists have affirmed an open ecclesiology which invites people to faith and discipleship regardless of where they are on the Christian journey; continuing reflection on whether the church can and should find ways to translate its nonviolent ethic in an effort to influence political and other secular institutions and structures is a topic for further research.

Another implication of the practical-theological dialogue is related to a potential objection to nonviolence posed by just war advocates—that nonviolence does not sufficiently consider and follow Jesus' teachings about love of one's neighbor. However this is a valid objection *only if* nonviolence is equated with a certain passive-ism in the face of such injustice. As the nonviolent United Methodist study participants make abundantly clear, their definition of nonviolence includes a very serious and active concern for justice and well-being of one's neighbor tempered by a Christ-centered unwillingness to use violence in order to attain these goals.[61] The lived theology vision of nonviolence as active and concerned

60. Frank, *Polity, Practice, and the Mission of the United Methodist Church*, 154, referencing Randy Maddox's work in "Social Grace: The Eclipse of the Church as a Means of Grace in American Methodism," in *Methodism in Its Cultural Milieu*, Proceedings of the Centenary Conference of the Wesley Historical Society (Oxford: Applied Theology, 1994), 147–49.

61. That current discourse about war and peace has failed to grasp this option is evident not only in the literature but showed up recently in a public lecture given by Catholic theologian J. Bryan Hehir, who argued that the only options for dealing with war morally in the modern world are 1) a return to a separatist passivity; 2) a version of classical realism that says the only moral objective in war is to finish it as quickly as possible (using virtually any means necessary) so that all can return to "normalcy"; and

for justice is absolutely essential here, for it reminds us that the choice is not between "doing nothing" or loving the neighbor through killing his oppressor—it is about nonviolent neighbor love which sees even the enemy as neighbor. The lived theology vision means working actively for the same things that just war wants (at its best) but limits that activity to nonviolent methods and means. If the church were to follow these implications out to their logical ends, it might even mean that Christians who adopt a Christ-centered nonviolence may be asked to engage in efforts for justice which put their very lives at risk.

Given the affirmation of an open and inclusive ecclesiology, nonviolence would not be considered a "rule" for the church nor a requirement of membership. Instead, it might be recognized as representing an ideal of Christian discipleship—a goal to which United Methodists should aspire as they move along the path to becoming better disciples. As such, the church—in its denominational, annual conference, and local church aspects—would have to make a conscious effort to nurture that ethic and to support those members who opt for nonviolence as a way of life.

How can the United Methodist Church help people to pursue such an ideal of discipleship? As Will Willimon declares succinctly, "Disciples are made, not born."[62] The process by which people become disciples is "so against the mainstream, so uncommon that nothing less than intentional, careful, Christian formation will do."[63] Formation, then, is centrally important to discussions about discipleship and a nonviolent ethic within the disciple's life. Formation cannot be relegated only to Sunday School and Christian Education programs, although those are both crucial areas in which formation occurs. Liturgy that emphasizes nonviolence and peacemaking through its prayers, hymns, preaching, and eucharistic practices is a crucial point of contact for the Christian community. Seminary education could include courses that challenge students to think about the connections between ethics and discipleship and which expose students to nonviolence as a Christian ethical option. In fact the academy could take on a specific role in formation toward discipleship which sees

---

3) a just war ethic, the objectives of which are based on justice. No concession was made for the possibility of a nonviolent ethic which sees justice as a crucial defining characteristic. J. Bryan Hehir, "Religion, Morality, and War" (lecture, Memorial Church of Harvard University, Cambridge, MA, March 15, 2007).

62. Willimon, *Why I Am a United Methodist*, 49.

63. Ibid., 48.

nonviolence as central; what would be tremendously helpful on the part of the academy is further development of the theological foundations and sources named by participants (particular biblical passages and themes, theologies of creation, resurrection, and eschatology, interpretations of the life and teachings of Jesus Christ) as theological underpinnings specifically of a nonviolent ethic. In addition, the academy can help the church to further consider what we *say* we believe and the actual implications of those beliefs for our ethical practices.

In efforts to nurture a nonviolent ethic in the church, the holding up of models of discipleship becomes an important practice. The church needs models to remind it of its goals of Christian discipleship. In many ways this study points to the need for such models through its lived theology emphasis, wherein the lives of people who embody a particular way of life invite and inspire others—in ways that current doctrinal statements are not able—to understand nonviolence more accurately and deeply and to live into a nonviolent lifestyle as a meaningful way of practicing discipleship. In the words of one study participant, "I believe that people that we encounter in the world are—some of them are very Jesus-like, and when I observe that, then I read the Scriptures with new eyes, and then I may . . . bring that to a situation" (P3). By making the lived theology of nonviolence explicit and available to others in the church, nonviolent United Methodists can challenge others to reflect on the meaning of discipleship and faith and to be able to recognize and learn from those who endeavor to pursue discipleship in their lives. If an open ecclesiology only succeeds if the church draws people along on the path of discipleship, then the capacity of a lived theology approach to point to models of discipleship can be an important way to support people along that path. In looking to and learning from others who are living out this particular path of discipleship, "United Methodists inherit a living tradition" as they draw "upon the experience of United Methodist people across the generations who also [seek] authentic ways to be the church."[64]

CONCLUSION

A number of the nonviolent United Methodists who were interviewed for this study articulated a call for the same thing: the facilitation of dialogue at the local, regional, and denominational levels of the United Methodist

---

64. Frank, *Polity, Practice, and the Mission of the United Methodist Church*, 114.

Church around questions of war, peace, and nonviolence and continued conversation about how the church might be faithful in dealing with such difficult moral issues. The guiding intention of this project has been to contribute to such dialogue within the United Methodist Church by drawing out the voices of those whose lives reflect and illustrate a particular path of discipleship to Jesus Christ through a nonviolent lifestyle and commitment and by allowing those voices to speak to the doctrine and thereby to the wider church itself. This study is offered as a hopeful contribution to such dialogue and discussion as the church continues to wrestle with how to answer the call to faithfulness around the moral issues of war and violence.

Afterword

THIS STUDY CONCLUDED IN the spring of 2007 and therefore does not include discussion of related proceedings from the 2008 General Conference of the United Methodist Church. A brief word about these proceedings is relevant and important for continued discussion of the issues raised by the study.

At the 2008 Conference, Howard Hallman, representing the organization Methodists United for Peace with Justice, submitted a petition to change the Social Principles statement on War and Peace. In the proposed statement, concessions to the just war principle of last resort were removed and specific scriptural references that point explicitly to the call to Christian discipleship were included in the third sentence of the proposal: "As disciples of Christ, we are called to love our enemies (Matt 4:43–48; Luke 23:34), reject the use of violence (Matt 5:38–39, 26:52; Luke 22:51), seek justice (Luke 4:16–21, Micah 6:8), and serve as reconcilers of conflict (2 Cor 5:17–18)."[1] Given the call by this study's participants for a clearer connection between discipleship, the call to nonviolence, and the Scripture references that participants themselves named as important to their own nonviolent commitments, this would have been a much-appreciated improvement indeed.

However, the legislative committee amended Hallman's petition in two interesting ways. First, the committee takes a firm stand against preemptive war in stating that "We oppose unilateral first/preemptive strike actions and strategies on the part of any government."[2] This is a statement that, one would imagine, most proponents of Christian nonviolence could certainly support. Perhaps more interesting is the fact that the legislative

---

1. Petition 80981, "General Conference 2008 Legislation Tracking." Online: http://calms.umc.org/2008/Menu.aspx?type=Petition&mode=Single&Number=80981.

2. Calendar Item 188, "Legislative Committee Report." Online: http://calms.umc.org/2008/Menu.aspx?type=Petition&mode=Single&Number=80981 (follow the link in the middle of the page to the Legistlative Committee's amendment of the petition).

committee chose to delete the parenthetical scriptural references in the sentence noted in the previous paragraph above. Why specific references to supporting Christian Scriptures were deemed unworthy of inclusion in the final adopted paragraph is unclear. Furthermore—and perhaps non-violent Methodist Christians would find this to be the most disturbing alteration of the proposed statement—the phrase calling on disciples of Christ to "reject the use of violence" seems to have disappeared, rather mysteriously, in the final version of the statement on War and Peace as it is printed in the 2008 *Book of Discipline*, which states only that "we are called to love our enemies, seek justice, and serve as reconcilers of conflict."[3] These unfortunate changes to the original proposal notwithstanding, at least the language (and even to some degree a description) of discipleship is retained in the paragraph.

Discussion of the Social Principles statement on Military Service also occurred at the 2008 General Conference. In another petition by Howard Hallman and Methodists United for Peace with Justice, several changes were suggested, three of which are particularly interesting in light of the previous study. First, Hallman added a sentence stating that "coercion, violence, and war" are to be rejected as "incompatible with the gospel and spirit of Christ."[4] This language is reflective of that articulated in Article XVI of the Evangelical United Brethren Confession of Faith (discussed extensively in chapter 4).

Second, Hallman's proposal drops several sentences that make concessions for belief and acceptance of both the just war and the pacifist stance within the United Methodist Church. With inclusion of the sentence above and rejection of the several sentences which indicate that either position is acceptable, the statement calls for a much firmer stance in favor of nonviolence. This is affirmed even more strongly in the third significant change suggested by Hallman, which drops the last sentence of the 2004 statement: "As Christians we are aware that neither the way of military action, nor the way of inaction is always righteous before God."[5] Unfortunately, however, the legislative committee rejected all three of

3. *Book of Discipline* (2008), 128–29.

4. Petition 80980, "General Conference 2008 Legislation Tracking." Online: http://calms.umc.org/2008/Menu.aspx?type=Petition&mode=Single&Number=80980.

5. Ibid. Discussion of this statement (and the objections to the wording included in it) is included in chapter 6, pages 113–14.

these proposed changes to the statement on Military Service,[6] thereby maintaining a statement of doctrinal teaching that many Methodist scholars have judged to be ambiguous, inconsistent, or otherwise unhelpful to a denomination wrestling with these very important moral issues.

At the very least, the discussions about doctrinal wording of Social Principles statements at the 2008 General Conference indicate that the issues raised by this study are alive and well and far from settled. Clearly, the people of the United Methodist Church must continue to wrestle with these questions through ongoing dialogue—in which all sides are heard and understood—and through continued, intentional steps toward ever-increasing faithfulness and discipleship.

6. Calendar Item 1, "Legislative Committee Report." Online: http://calms.umc.org /2008/Menu.aspx?type=Petition&mode=Single&Number=80980 (follow the link in the middle of the page to the Legistlative Committee's amendment of the petition).

Appendix A

Informed Consent Form

Topic of Research Project: Understanding the Lived Theology of Contemporary United Methodist Christians Who Are Committed to Nonviolence

Researcher: Nicole (Niki) Johnson (njohnson@bu.edu; 617.780.7617)
Advisors: Dr. Claire E. Wolfteich (cwolftei@bu.edu; 617.353.6496) and
Dr. Dale P. Andrews (andrews@bu.edu; 617.353.3050)

My name is Niki Johnson, and I am a candidate for the Doctor of Theology degree in Practical Theology at Boston University School of Theology. As part of my doctoral dissertation, I am conducting research on the practices, values, ideals, and principles (or "lived theology") of nonviolence in the lives of United Methodist Christians who hold a commitment to nonviolence as central to Christian faith.

As part of this research project, I am interviewing United Methodists who identify themselves and who can be identified by others as having a commitment to nonviolence. Interviewees have been identified through methods of "chain-sampling" and organizations devoted to nonviolence. By agreeing to volunteer for this study, you are agreeing to an approximately one-hour interview which will be audio-recorded and will involve questions about how you understand your commitment to nonviolence, how that commitment is lived and practiced in your life and work, and what sources serve to guide and sustain the commitment to nonviolence. This interview will be conducted in-person at a location that is convenient for you. I do not expect your participation in this study to put you at any risk; however, should you feel uncomfortable during the interview, you are welcome to discuss any concerns or questions with me or with the advisors. We are also available to answer any questions about the research generally. This study is voluntary; you are not required to answer every question and you may withdraw from the study at any time with no penalties. In this case, any data connected with your interview will be destroyed. I do expect that you may benefit from involvement in this study in that it will offer you an opportunity to reflect on your faith journey and your commitment to nonviolence.

The recorded interview will be transcribed, analyzed, and interpreted. All data will be kept confidential; tapes and transcript copies will be kept under lock and key, and tapes will be destroyed at the conclusion of the project. Any portions of the interview quoted in the final project will be acknowledged only by demographic indicators.

If you have any questions about your rights as a participant in this study, you may contact David Berndt (Senior Associate Director, Institutional Review Board) at (617) 353-4365. For general questions about the project, Professor Wolfteich can be reached at cwolftei@bu.edu, (617) 353-6496 and Professor Andrews can be reached at andrews@bu.edu, (617) 353-3050. You may contact me at any time at njohnson@bu.edu, (617) 780-7617.

Thank you for your participation in this study.

I, the undersigned, have read the above. My signature gives consent to being interviewed for the purposes described above. The interview will be tape-recorded and transcribed. My mailing address is included below for a copy of this signed consent form.

Date: _____

Signature: _____

Name (please print): _____

Address: _____

_____

Signature for permission
to tape record: _____

Person obtaining consent: _____

APPENDIX B

Interview Aid

Name:
Age:
Residence:
Occupation:
Lay/Clergy status:
Years in the UMC:
Racial/ethnic identity:
Social-economic class of origin:
Social-economic class at present:
Today's date:

1. In just a sentence or two, how would you define nonviolence?

2. What are the most central Scriptural passages or theological concepts in your commitment to nonviolence?

3. What are your "practices" of nonviolence—the things you do that would reveal to others that you are nonviolent and/or that help you to sustain that commitment?

4. What is the "official" doctrine or teaching of the United Methodist Church regarding how we should respond to war and violence? Briefly summarize what you know or believe to be the teachings of the church.

Appendix C

Interview Grid

Interviewee Name:
Date:
__ Informed Consent Form
__ Interview Aid

What is the lived theology of United Methodist Christians who are committed to nonviolence, and what sustains that commitment? How might a lived theology of nonviolence speak to a denomination that maintains a plurality of teachings within its doctrinal tradition?

1. (5) Entry

- Why do you think others have identified you as someone who would be good for this study?

- Do you remember the first time you felt you had a commitment to nonviolence? Tell me when that occurred and then tell me more about that.

2. (5) How do United Methodists define and understand their commitments to non-violence?

- In just a few sentences, how would you define nonviolence as *you* understand and live it?

- When you hear the word "non-violence," what does that mean to you?

- How do you understand your commitment to non-violence?

- Is there a difference between non-violence and Christian non-violence for you? If so, tell me about that difference.

3. (10) What theological (and other) sources and/or theories undergird the commitment to non-violence?

- Is there one Scripture passage(s) that is most central to you in your commitment to non-violence? Why and how is this passage important to you?

- Is there a central driving theological concept or idea(s) that you continually return to when you are looking for empowerment to stay non-violent?

- Are there any other ideas that you might not classify as particularly "Christian" or theological or church-oriented but that are really important for you in the way you go about being non-violent?

4. (10) What are the practices of nonviolence among United Methodists who have that commitment [that sustain the commitment to non-violence]?

- What are the things you *do* or the practices in which you engage that make you a non-violent person?

- How, if at all, has the actual practice and work of non-violence changed what you believe about non-violence?

- In other words, do you think that the practices you have named serve to reinforce your commitment – that by doing them your commitment actually grows stronger? How so?

- Name one or two things you do that are central to what it means for you to be non-violent. Why is this/are these important?

5. (10) How are United Methodists formed toward non-violence?

- Has your involvement in the UMC made a difference for your formation and identity as a non-violent person? How so? Can you give me an example of how the church has influenced you?

- What ministries of the United Methodist Church, such as worship, religious education, fellowship, small groups, etc, have influenced your formation toward non-violence?

- How do you think you arrived at having this commitment and being sufficiently involved in it that others would name/identify you as having this commitment?

- What or who has had the biggest influence on you in your journey toward non-violence?

- What has your journey toward non-violence looked like?

6. (10) How do United Methodists view the UMC teachings on war, peace, and non-violence?

- What are the basic teachings about war, peace, and non-violence that stand out for you or that you are familiar with in the *Book of Discipline* and/or the *Book of Resolutions*?

- If you could, and if you wanted to do so, how would you re-write the teachings on war, peace, and non-violence in the *Book of Discipline* and/or the *Book of Resolutions*? (transition question to next section ...)

- What does the *Book of Discipline* say about war, peace, and non-violence? Has it been important to you to be aware of these teachings?

- When did you first learn about the teachings of the UMC? How were they communicated to you?

- What are your thoughts about the teachings? Do you find them helpful?

7. (10+) How do non-violent Methodists sustain the commitment to non-violence?

- Have you ever felt any tension between being a non-violent person and being a United Methodist? Can you give me an example?

- Do you ever think about leaving the UMC and joining, for example, one of the historic peace churches? Tell me about that.

- How do you sustain the commitment to nonviolence in a violent world, particularly as a Methodist?

8. Closure

- Are there any other comments or thoughts related to any of the topics we have covered in this interview that you would like to share with me as we bring this interview to a close?

Bibliography

Abraham, William J. *Waking from Doctrinal Amnesia: The Healing of Doctrine in the United Methodist Church*. Nashville: Abingdon, 1995.

Allen, Joseph L. *War: A Primer for Christians*. 1st Maquire Center/SMU Press ed. Dallas: Cary M. Maguire Center for Ethics and Public Responsibility, Southern Methodist University Press, 2000.

Ammerman, Nancy T. "Introduction." In *Everyday Religion: Observing Modern Religious Lives*, ed. Nancy T. Ammerman, 3–20. New York: Oxford University Press, 2007.

———, editor. *Everyday Religion: Observing Modern Religious Lives*. New York: Oxford University Press, 2007.

Arendt, Hannah. *On Violence*. New York: Harcourt, Brace, and World, 1970.

Bainton, Roland. *Christian Attitudes Toward War and Peace: A Historical Survey and Critical Re-Evaluation*. Nashville: Abingdon, 1960.

Ballou, Adin. *Christian Non-Resistance in All Its Important Bearings*. New York: De Capo, 1970.

Battle, Michael. *Blessed Are the Peacemakers: A Christian Spirituality of Nonviolence*. Macon, GA: Mercer University Press, 2004.

Behney, J. Bruce, and Paul H. Eller. *The History of the Evangelical United Brethren Church*. Edited by Kenneth W. Krueger. Nashville: Abingdon, 1979.

Berger, Peter L. "Foreword." In *Everyday Religion: Observing Modern Religious Lives*, ed. Nancy T. Ammerman, v–x. New York: Oxford University Press, 2007.

Board of Bishops, Evangelical United Brethren Church. *The Episcopal Message to the General Conference*. Chicago: Board of Bishops of the Evangelical United Brethren Church, 1966.

Board of Christian Education and the Board of Evangelism, Evangelical United Brethren Church. *This We Believe: A Commentary on the Confession of Faith of the Evangelical United Brethren Church*. Dayton, OH: The Board of Christian Education of the Evangelical United Brethren Church, 1964.

Boff, Leonardo. *Ecclesiogenesis: The Base Communities Reinvent the Church*. Maryknoll, NY: Orbis, 1986.

Book of Discipline of the United Methodist Church. Nashville: United Methodist Publishing House, 1968–2004 editions.

Book of Resolutions of the United Methodist Church. Nashville: United Methodist Publishing House, 1968–2004 editions.

Boring, M. Eugene. *The Continuing Voice of Jesus: Christian Prophecy and the Gospel Tradition*. Louisville: Westminster John Knox, 1991.

Boulding, Elise. *Cultures of Peace: The Hidden Side of History*. Syracuse, NY: Syracuse University Press, 2000.

Brimlow, Robert W. *What about Hitler? Wrestling with Jesus's Call to Nonviolence in an Evil World.* The Christian Practice of Everyday Life Series. Grand Rapids: Brazos, 2006.

Brown, Robert McAfee. *Religion and Violence.* 2nd ed. Philadelphia: Westminster, 1987.

———. Review of *Non-Violence, Central to Christian Spirituality,* ed. by Joseph Culliton. *Journal of Ecumenical Studies* 22 (1985) 152–53.

Browning, Don S. *A Fundamental Practical Theology: Descriptive and Strategic Proposals.* Minneapolis: Fortress, 1991.

———. *Practical Theology: The Emerging Field in Theology, Church, and World.* San Francisco: Harper & Row, 1983.

———. "Toward a Fundamental and Strategic Practical Theology." In *Shifting Boundaries: Contextual Approaches to the Structure of Theological Education,* ed. Barbara Wheeler and Edward Farley, 295–328. Louisville: Westminster John Knox, 1991.

Brueggemann, Walter. *The Prophetic Imagination.* Minneapolis: Fortress, 1978.

Buthelezi, Manas. "The Church as a Prophetic Sign." In *Church, Kingdom, World: The Church as Mystery and Prophetic Sign,* ed. Gennadios Limouris, 138–44. Faith and Order Paper No. 130, World Council of Churches, Geneva. Geneva, Switzerland: World Council of Churches, 1986.

Cahill, Lisa Sowle. *Love Your Enemies: Discipleship, Pacifism, and Just War Theory.* Minneapolis: Fortress, 1994.

———. "Theological Contexts of Just War Theory and Pacifism: A Response to J. Bryan Hehir." *Journal of Religious Ethics* 20 (1992) 259–65.

Campbell, Dennis, William Lawrence, and Russell Richey, editors. *Doctrines and Discipline.* Nashville: Abingdon, 1999.

Campbell, Ted. *Methodist Doctrine: The Essentials.* Nashville: Abingdon, 1999.

Carmody, Denise Lardner, and John Tully Carmody, editors. *The Future of Prophetic Christianity: Essays in Honor of Robert McAfee Brown.* Maryknoll, NY: Orbis, 1993.

Carter, April, David Hoggett, and Adam Roberts. *Non-violent Action: A Selected Bibliography.* Haverford, PA: Center for Nonviolent Conflict Resolution, Haverford College, 1970.

Childress, James. "Just War Criteria." In *War or Peace? The Search for New Answers,* ed. Thomas A. Shannon, 40–58. Maryknoll, NY: Orbis, 1982.

Cobb, John B. "Is Theological Pluralism Dead in the U.M.C.?" In *Doctrine and Theology in the United Methodist Church,* ed. Thomas A. Langford, 162–67. Nashville: Abingdon, 1991.

Cobb, John B., and Joseph Hough. *Christian Identity and Theological Education.* Atlanta: Scholar's, 1985.

Collins, John Joseph. *Does the Bible Justify Violence?* Minneapolis: Fortress, 2004.

Corbett, Jack Elliott, and Elizabeth Smith. *Becoming a Prophetic Community.* Atlanta: John Knox, 1980.

Creswell, John W. *Qualitative Inquiry and Research Design: Choosing Among Five Traditions.* Thousand Oaks, CA: Sage, 1998.

Culliton, Joseph T., editor. *Non-Violence, Central to Christian Spirituality: Perspectives from Scripture to the Present.* New York: Mellen, 1982.

Cushman, Robert E. *John Wesley's Experimental Divinity: Studies in Methodist Doctrinal Standards.* Nashville: Kingswood, 1989.

Darling, Dallas. "To Follow the Way of Peace." *Christian Social Action* 4 (1991) 34–35.

Deats, Paul, editor. *Toward a Discipline of Social Ethics: Essays in Honor of Walter George Muelder.* Boston: Boston University Press, 1972.

Deats, Paul, and Herbert Stotts. *Methodism and Society: Guidelines for Strategy*. Edited by the Board of Social and Economic Relations of the Methodist Church. New York: Abingdon, 1962.

Deats, Richard. *Martin Luther King, Jr., Spirit-Led Prophet: A Biography*. Hyde Park, NY: New City, 1999.

Douglass, James W. *The Non-Violent Cross: A Theology of Revolution and Peace*. 1968. Reprint, Eugene, OR: Wipf & Stock, 2006.

Durnbaugh, Donald F. "Counting the Cost of Peace." *Brethren Life and Thought* 32 (1987) 53–62.

Dykstra, Craig. *Growing in the Life of Faith: Education and Christian Practices*. 2nd ed. Louisville, Kentucky: Westminster John Knox, 2005.

Fahey, Joseph, and Richard Armstrong, editors. *A Peace Reader: Essential Readings on War, Justice, Non-Violence, and World Order*. Mahwah, NJ: Paulist, 1992.

Farley, Edward. "Protestant Practical Theology." In *Dictionary of Pastoral Care and Counseling*, ed. Rodney Hunter et al., 934–36. Nashville, TN: Abingdon, 1990.

————. *Theologia: The Fragmentation and Unity of Theological Education*. 1994. Reprint, Eugene, OR: Wipf & Stock, 2001.

Felton, Gayle C., editor. *How United Methodists Study Scripture*. Nashville: Abingdon, 1999.

Finn, James. "Pacifism and Justifiable War." In *War or Peace? The Search for New Answers*, ed. Thomas A. Shannon, 3–14. Maryknoll, NY: Orbis, 1982.

Frank, Thomas Edward. *Polity, Practice, and the Mission of the United Methodist Church*. Nashville: Abingdon, 2002.

Gill, David. "Violence and Non-Violence: Resuming the Debate." *Ecumenical Review* 32 (1980) 25–29.

Graham, Elaine. *Transforming Practice: Pastoral Theology in an Age of Uncertainty*. 1996. Reprint, Eugene, OR: Wipf & Stock, 2002.

Groome, Thomas. *Christian Religious Education*. San Francisco: Jossey-Bass, 1980.

Guder, Darell, editor. *The Missional Church: A Vision for the Sending of the Church in North America*. Grand Rapids: Eerdmans, 1998.

Hakola, Gretchen. "Social Justice, Human Rights, Peace . . . What Would Jesus Do?" *Christian Social Action* 13.2 (2000) 4–13.

Hall, David D., editor. *Lived Religion in America: Toward a History of Practice*. Princeton: Princeton University Press, 1997.

Hammond, David M., editor. *Theology and Lived Christianity*. Annual Publication of the College Theology Society 45. Mystic, CT: Twenty-Third Publications, 2000.

Hauerwas, Stanley. *Against the Nations: War and Survival in a Liberal Society*. Minneapolis: Winston, 1985.

————. *A Better Hope: Resources for a Church Confronting Capitalism, Democracy, and Postmodernity*. Grand Rapids: Brazos, 2000.

————. *Dispatches from the Front: Theological Engagements with the Secular*. Durham, NC: Duke University Press, 1994.

————. "Epilogue: A Pacifist Response to the Bishops." In *Speak up for Just War or Pacifism: A Critique of the United Methodist Bishops' Pastoral Letter 'In Defense of Creation,'* Paul Ramsey, 149–82. University Park: Pennsylvania State University Press, 1988.

————. *In Good Company: The Church as Polis*. Notre Dame, IN: University of Notre Dame Press, 1995.

———. "Jesus and the Social Embodiment of the Peaceable Kingdom (1983)." In *The Hauerwas Reader*, ed. John Berkman and Michael Cartwright, 116–41. Durham, NC: Duke University Press, 2001.

———. *The Peaceable Kingdom: A Primer for Christian Ethics.* Notre Dame, IN: University of Notre Dame Press, 1984.

———. "The Servant Community: Christian Social Ethics (1983)." In *The Hauerwas Reader*, ed. John Berkman and Michael Cartwright, 371–91. Durham, NC: Duke University Press, 2001.

———. *Vision and Virtue: Essays in Christian Ethical Reflection.* Notre Dame, IN: Fides, 1974.

———. "Why Gays (as a Group) Are Morally Superior to Christians (as a Group)." In *The Hauerwas Reader*, ed. John Berkman and Michael Cartwright, 519–21. Durham, NC: Duke University Press, 2001.

Hauerwas, Stanley, Linda Hogan, and Enda McDonagh. "The Case for the Abolition of War in the Twenty-First Century." *Journal of the Society of Christian Ethics* 25.2 (2005) 17–35.

Hays, Richard. *The Moral Vision of the New Testament: Community, Cross, New Creation; A Contemporary Introduction to New Testament Ethics.* San Francisco, HarperSanFrancisco, 1996.

Hehir, J. Bryan. "The Just-War Ethic." In *War or Peace? The Search for New Answers*, ed. Thomas A. Shannon, 15–39. Maryknoll, NY: Orbis, 1982.

———. "Just War Theory in a Post-Cold War World." *Journal of Religious Ethics* 20 (1992) 237–57.

Heimbrock, Hans-Gunter. "Given through the Senses: A Phenomenological Model of Empirical Theology." In *Normativity and Empirical Research in Theology*, ed. Johannes A. Van der Ven and Michael Scherer-Rath, 59–84. Leiden: Brill, 2004.

Hempton, David. *Methodism: Empire of the Spirit.* New Haven, CT: Yale University Press, 2005.

Heschel, Abraham J. *The Prophets.* New York: Harper & Row, 1962.

Hodapp, Bishop Leroy. "Foreword." In *A Will for Peace: Peace Action in the United Methodist Church: A History*, by Herman Will, vii–ix. Washington DC: General Board of Church and Society of the United Methodist Church, 1984.

Holland, Scott. "The Gospel of Peace and the Violence of God." In *Seeking Cultures of Peace: A Peace Church Conversation*, ed. Fernando Enns, Scott Holland, and Ann Rigs, 132–46, Scottdale, PA: Herald, 2004.

Horsley, Richard A. "Ethics and Exegesis: 'Love Your Enemies' and the Doctrine of Non-Violence." *Journal of the American Academy of Religion* 54 (1986) 3–31.

Howell, Leon. *United Methodism at Risk: A Wake-Up Call.* Kingston, NY: Information Project for United Methodists, 2003.

Hunsberger, George R., et al., editors. *The Church Between Gospel and Culture.* Grand Rapids: Eerdmans, 1996.

Isazi-Diaz, Ada Maria. *Mujerista Theology: A Theology for the Twenty-First Century.* Maryknoll, NY: Orbis, 1996.

Johnson, James Turner. "Just War." In *The Westminster Dictionary of Christian Ethics*, ed. James F. Childress and John Macquarrie, 328–29. Philadelphia: Westminster, 1986.

———. *Morality and Contemporary Warfare.* New Haven, CT: Yale University Press, 1999.

Joint Commissions on Church Union of The United Methodist Church and The Evangelical United Brethren Church. *The Constitution of The United Methodist Church (with Enabling Legislation and Other Historic Documents).* United States of America: Donald A. Theuer for the Joint Commissions on Church Union of The Methodist Church and The Evangelical United Brethren Church, 1967.

Jones, Scott. *United Methodist Doctrine: The Extreme Center.* Nashville: Abingdon, 2002.

Journal of the 1972 General Conference of the United Methodist Church, vol. 1. 16–28 April 1972. Atlanta: The United Methodist Church, 1972.

Journal of the 1980 General Conference of the United Methodist Church, vol. 1. 15–25 April 1980. Indianapolis: The United Methodist Church, 1980.

Journal of the 2000 General Conference of the United Methodist Church, vols. 1 & 4. 2–13 May 2000. Cleveland: The United Methodist Church, 2000.

Keegan, John E. "Christian Martyrdom and the Transformation of the World: Martin Luther King, Jr." *Saint Luke's Journal of Theology* 26 (1983) 195–211.

Kepple, David. "West Ohio United Methodists Address Non-Violence." *Christian Social Action* 14.2 (2001) 23–24.

Kirk-Duggan, Cheryl A. *Violence and Theology.* Nashville: Abingdon, 2006.

Knight, Henry H., and Don E. Saliers. *The Conversation Matters: Why United Methodists Should Talk with One Another.* Nashville: Abingdon, 1999.

Koning, Hans. "Notes on the Twentieth Century." *The Atlantic Monthly* 280.3 (1997) 90–100.

Krueger, Kenneth W, editor. *The History of the Evangelical United Brethren Church.* Nashville: Abingdon, 1979.

Küng, Hans, and Jürgen Moltmann, editors. *A Council for Peace.* Edinburgh: T. & T. Clark, 1988.

Lacy, Hugh. "The Harsh Choice: Facing Systemic Violece." *Other Side* 22.9 (1986) 24–25.

Langford, Thomas A., editor. *Doctrine and Theology in the United Methodist Church.* Nashville: Abingdon, 1991.

Lathrop, Gordon. *Holy People: A Liturgical Ecclesiology.* Minneapolis: Fortress, 1999.

Lederach, John Paul. *Building Peace: Sustainable Reconciliation in Divided Societies.* Washington DC: United States Institute of Peace Press, 1997.

———. *Preparing for Peace: Conflict Transformation across Cultures.* Syracuse, NY: Syracuse University Press, 1995.

Lewis, Dean H. "Participation in Violation." *Church & Society* 64 (1974) 5–53.

Lohfink, Gerhard. *Does God Need the Church? Toward a Theology of the People of God.* Translated by Linda M. Maloney. Collegeville, MN: Liturgical, 1999.

Long, D. Stephen. *Living the Discipline: United Methodist Theological Reflections on War, Civilization, and Holiness.* Grand Rapids: Eerdmans, 1992.

Maddox, Randy L. "Practical Theology: A Discipline in Search of a Definition." *Perspectives in Religious Studies* 18 (1991) 159–69.

Madsen, Norman. *This We Believe: The Articles of Religion and the Confession of Faith of the United Methodist Church.* Nashville: Graded, 1987.

Mahoney, Roger. "The Eucharist and Social Justice." *Worship* 57 (1983) 52–61.

Mauser, Ulrich. *The Gospel of Peace: A Scriptural Message for Today's World.* Louisville: Westminster John Knox, 1992.

Meeks, M. Douglas, and Robert D. Mutton, editors. *In Essentials Unity: Reflections on the Nature and Purpose of the Church: In Honor of Frederick R. Trost.* Minneapolis: Kirk House, 2001.

Merton, Thomas. *The Nonviolent Alternative*. Edited by Gordon C. Zahn. New York: Farrar, Straus and Giroux, 1980.

Milbank, John. *Theology and Social Theory: Beyond Secular Reason*. Oxford: Blackwell, 1990.

Miller, Richard B. "Pacifism and Just War Tenets: How Do They Diverge?" *Theological Studies* 47 (1986) 448–72.

Moberly, R.W.L. *Prophecy and Discernment*. Cambridge: Cambridge University Press, 2006.

Moon, Dawne. *God, Sex, and Politics: Homosexuality and Everyday Theologies*. Chicago: University of Chicago Press, 2004.

Moore, Peter C. *A Church to Believe In*. Solon, OH: Latimer, 1994.

Muelder, Walter. "Critical Reflections on 'Violence, Non-Violence and the Struggle for Justice.'" In *Selected Papers: Seventeenth Annual Meeting—the American Society of Christian Ethics*, ed. Max L. Stackhouse. Atlanta: Scholars, 1976.

———. "The Methodist Social Creed and Ecumenical Ethics." In *Wesleyan Theology Today: A Bicentennial Theological Consultation*. Edited by Theodore Runyon. Nashville: Kingswood, 1985.

———. *Methodism and Society in the Twentieth Century*. Edited by the Board of Social and Economic Relations of the Methodist Church. Nashville: Abingdon, 1961.

Muste, Abraham John. *Non-Violence in an Aggressive World*. New York: Harper, 1940.

Neal, Christie. "Building Bridges and Bridging the Gaps: How Do We Live as Peace-Makers in a Violent World?" *Christian Social Action* 12 (1999) 4–5.

Neville, David, and Philip Matthews, editors. *Faith and Freedom: Christian Ethics in a Pluralist Culture*. Adelaide: ATF, 2003.

O'Brien, William. "A Way in the World: The Spiritual Revolution of Nonviolence." *Other Side* 22.9 (1986) 16–22.

Oden, Thomas C. *Doctrinal Standards in the Wesleyan Tradition*. Grand Rapids: Asbury, 1988.

Orsi, Robert. "Everyday Miracles: The Study of Lived Religion." In *Lived Religion in America: Toward a History of Practice*, ed. David D. Hall, 3–21. Princeton: Princeton University Press, 1997.

Outler, Albert C. "Introduction to the Report of the 1968–72 Theological Study Commission." In *Doctrine and Theology in the United Methodist Church*, ed. Thomas A. Langford, 20–25. Nashville: Abingdon, 1991.

Panikkar, Raimundo. *Cultural Disarmament: The Way to Peace*. Translated by Robert R. Barr. Louisville: Westminster John Knox, 1995.

Parks, S. Ronald. "Free (but Not Helped) to Be Pacifist: Methodist COs in the Vietnam Era." In *Proclaim Peace: Christian Pacifism from Unexpected Quarters*, ed. Theron F. Schlabach and Richard T. Hughes, 204–16. Urbana and Chicago: University of Illinois Press, 1997.

Patton, Michael Quinn. *Qualitative Research and Evaluation Methods*, 3rd ed. Thousand Oaks, CA: Sage, 2002.

"Peace Forum." *Christian Social Action* 1 (1988) 27.

Poling, James, and Donald Miller. *Foundations for a Practical Theology of Ministry*. Nashville: Abingdon, 1985.

Price, Elizabeth Box, and Charles R. Price, editors. *By What Authority: A Conversation on Teaching among United Methodists*. Nashville: Abingdon, 1991.

Ramsey, Paul. *The Just War: Force and Political Responsibility*. New York: Scribners, 1968.

————. *Speak Up for Just War of Pacifism: A Critique of the United Methodist Bishops' Pastoral Letter "In Defense of Creation."* University Park: Pennsylvania State University Press, 1988.

————. *War and the Christian Conscience: How Shall Modern War Be Conducted Justly?* Durham, NC: Duke University Press, 1961.

Ramseyer, Robert L., editor. *Mission and the Peace Witness: The Gospel and Christian Discipleship.* Scottdale, PA: Herald, 1979.

Ranck, Lee. "Rivers in the Desert." *Christian Social Action* 8 (1995) 4–16, 25–36.

————. "Worship Resources." *Christian Social Action* 3 (1990) 4–14, 20–22.

The Random House College Dictionary. Revised Edition. New York: Random House, 1988.

Ray, Ritendra K., editor. *Gandhi and King: Dialogue on Non-Violence.* Toronto: Gandhi and King Conference Committee, 1993.

Richey, Russell E., Dennis M. Campbell, and William B. Lawrence, editors. *Connectionalism: Ecclesiology, Mission, and Identity.* Nashville: Abingdon, 1997.

Rieger, Joerg, and John J. Vincent, editors. *Methodist and Radical: Rejuvenating a Tradition.* Nashville: Kingswood, 2003.

Riemer, Neal, editor. *Let Justice Roll: Prophetic Challenges in Religion, Politics, and Society.* Lanham, MD: Rowman and Littlefield, 1996.

Roth, John D. *Choosing Against War: A Christian View.* Intercourse, PA: Good Books, 2002.

Rowe, Kenneth. *United Methodist Studies: Basic Bibliographies.* Nashville: Abingdon, 1998.

Sample, Tex. "To Counter Violence in the World: Where are the Worship Centers of Non-Violence in Contrast to John Wayne, Clint Eastwood, Rambo, and Terminator 2?" *Christian Social Action* 8 (1995) 12–15.

Sanders, John, editor. *Atonement and Violence: A Theological Conversation.* Nashville: Abingdon, 2006.

Schleiermacher, Friedrich. *Brief Outline of the Study of Theology.* Translated by Terrence N. Tice. Richmond: John Knox, 1966.

Schomer, Howard. "Christian Non-Violence in the Nuclear Age." *Social Action* (US) 26 (1959) 10–17.

Schreiter, Robert J. *The New Catholicity: Theology Between the Global and the Local.* Maryknoll, NY: Orbis, 1997.

Sexton, Virgil Wesley. *Listening to the Church: A Realistic Profile of Grass Roots Opinion.* Nashville: Abingdon, 1971.

Shannon, Thomas, editor. *War or Peace? The Search for New Answers.* Maryknoll, NY: Orbis, 1982.

Sharp, Gene. *Waging Nonviolent Struggle: 20th Century Practice and 21st Century Potential.* Boston: Extending Horizons, Porter Sargent, 2005.

Sider, Ronald. *Christ and Violence.* Scottdale, PA: Herald, 1979.

————. *Non-Violence: The Invincible Weapon?* Dallas: Word, 1989.

Sprecher, Steven J. "Beyond Terrorism." *Christian Social Action* 14.6 (2001) 3–5.

Stackhouse, Max, editor. "Responding to the Sermon on the Mount." *Bangalore Theological Forum* 17 (1985) 1–97.

Stassen, Glen H. "Concrete Christological Norms for Transformation." In *Authentic Transformation: A New Vision of Christ and Culture*, ed. Glen H. Stassen, D. M. Yeager, and John Howard Yoder, 127–89. Nashville: Abingdon, 1996.

————. *Living the Sermon on the Mount: A Practical Hope for Grace and Deliverance.* Enduring Questions in Christian Life Series. San Francisco: Jossey-Bass, 2006.

————, editor. *Just Peacemaking: Ten Practices for Abolishing War.* Cleveland: Pilgrim, 1998.

Stassen, Glen H., and David P. Gushee. *Kingdom Ethics: Following Jesus in Contemporary Context.* Downers Grove, IL: InterVarsity, 2003.

Stassen, Glen H., D. M. Yeager, and John Howard Yoder. *Authentic Transformation: A New Vision of Christ and Culture.* Nashville: Abingdon, 1996.

Storey, Peter. *With God in the Crucible: Preaching Costly Discipleship.* Nashville: Abingdon, 2002.

Susin, Luiz Carlos, and Maria Pila Aquino, editors. *Reconciliation in a World of Conflicts.* London: SCM, 2003.

Sweet, William Warren. *Methodism in American History.* New York: Abingdon, 1953.

Swinton, John, and Harriet Mowat. *Practical Theology and Qualitative Research.* London: SCM, 2006.

Swomley, John. *Confronting Systems of Violence: Memoirs of a Peace Activist.* Nyack, NY: Fellowship Publications, 1998.

Tuell, Jack. *The Organization of the United Methodist Church.* Nashville: Abingdon, 2002.

United Methodist Council of Bishops. *In Defense of Creation: The Nuclear Crisis and a Just Peace.* Nashville: Graded, 1986.

United States Catholic Bishops. *The Challenge of Peace: God's Promise and Our Response.* In *Catholic Social Thought: The Documentary Heritage,* ed. David J. O'Brien and Thomas A. Shannon, 492–571. Maryknoll, NY: Orbis, 1992.

Veling, Terry A. *Practical Theology: "On Earth as It Is in Heaven."* Maryknoll, NY: Orbis, 2005.

Volf, Miroslav. *Exclusion and Embrace: A Theological Exploration of Identity, Otherness, and Reconciliation.* Nashville: Abingdon, 1996.

Volf, Miroslav, and Dorothy Bass, editors. *Practicing Theology: Beliefs and Practices in Christian Life.* Grand Rapids: Eerdmans, 2002.

Wagner, Rodney L. *The Development of Teaching Doctrines, Materials, and Institutions in the Evangelical United Brethren Church.* Documents Selected and Prepared by Rodney L. Wagner and others. Dayton, OH, 1963.

Wallis, Jim. *God's Politics: Why the Right Gets It Wrong and the Left Doesn't Get It.* New York: HarperCollins, 2005.

————, editor. *The Rise of Christian Conscience: The Emergence of a Dramatic Renewal Movement in the Church Today.* San Francisco: Harper & Row, 1987.

Waltz, Alan K. *A Dictionary for United Methodists.* Nashville: Abingdon, 1991.

Weaver, J. Denny. *The Nonviolent Atonement.* Grand Rapids: Eerdmans, 2001.

Wesley, John. "Of the Church." In *Sermons and Hymns of John Wesley* (CD-ROM). Edited by Richard P. Heitzenrater. Nashville: Abingdon, 1999.

Wheeler, Barbara, and Edward Farley, editors. *Shifting Boundaries: Contextual Approaches to the Structure of Theological Education.* Louisville: Westminster John Knox, 1991.

White, C. Dale. *Making a Just Peace: Human Rights and Domination Systems.* Nashville: Abingdon, 1998.

Will, Herman. "Peace Is the Way." *Christian Social Action* 6 (1993) 4–7.

————. *A Will for Peace: Peace Action in the United Methodist Church, A History.* Washington DC: General Board of Church and Society of the United Methodist Church, 1984.

Willimon, William H. *Why I Am a United Methodist*. Nashville: Abingdon, 1990.

Willimon, William H., and Stanley Hauerwas. *Lord Teach Us: The Lord's Prayer & the Christian Life*. With Scott C. Saye. Nashville: Abingdon, 1996.

Wink, Walter. *Jesus and Nonviolence: A Third Way*. Facets. Fortress, 2003.

———. *The Powers That Be: Theology for a New Millenium*. New York: Doubleday, 1998.

Wogaman, J. Philip. *To Serve the Present Age: The Gift and Promise of United Methodism*. Nashville: Abingdon, 1995.

———. "Shalom: The Theological Vision of Peace and Justice." *Christian Social Action* 2 (1989) 4–6.

Woodward, James, and Stephen Patterson, editors. *The Blackwell Reader in Pastoral and Practical Theology*. Oxford: Blackwell, 2000.

Yoder, John Howard. *Body Politics*. Nashville: Discipleship Resources, 1992.

———. *Christian Attitudes to War, Peace, and Revolution: A Companion to Bainton*. Elkhart, IN: Co-op Bookstore, 1983.

———. *The Christian Witness to the State*. Newton, KS: Faith and Life, 1964.

———. *For the Nations: Essays Evangelical and Public*. 1997. Reprint, Eugene, OR: Wipf & Stock, 2002.

———. *Nevertheless: The Varieties and Shortcomings of Religious Pacifism*. Scottdale, PA, 1976.

———. *The Original Revolution: Essays on Christian Pacifism*. Scottdale, PA: Herald, 1972.

———. *The Politics of Jesus*. 2nd ed. Grand Rapids: Eerdmans, 1994.

Yrigoyen, Charles. *Belief Matters: United Methodism's Doctrinal Standards*. Nashville: Abingdon, 2001.